55 BUDGET RECIPES FOR FAMILY MEALS

55 BUDGET RECIPES
FOR FAMILY MEALS

Delicious, nutritious and economical dishes shown
step by step in 280 fabulous colour photographs

Lucy Doncaster

HERMES
HOUSE

This edition is published by Hermes House,
an imprint of Anness Publishing Ltd, Hermes House,
88–89 Blackfriars Road, London SE1 8HA
tel. 020 7401 2077; fax 020 7633 9499

www.hermeshouse.com; www.annesspublishing.com

If you like the images in this book and would like to investigate using
them for publishing, promotions or advertising, please visit our website
www.practicalpictures.com for more information.

Publisher: Joanna Lorenz
Senior Managing Editor: Conor Kilgallon
Project Editor: Lucy Doncaster
Design: Paul Oakley Associates
Production Controller: Claire Rae

ETHICAL TRADING POLICY
Because of our ongoing ecological investment programme, you, as our customer,
can have the pleasure and reassurance of knowing that a tree is being cultivated on
your behalf to naturally replace the materials used to make the book you are
holding. For further information about this scheme, go to
www.annesspublishing.com/trees

PUBLISHER'S NOTE
Although the advice and information in this book are believed to be accurate and
true at the time of going to press, neither the authors nor the publisher can accept
any legal responsibility or liability for any errors or omissions that may be made nor
for any inaccuracies nor for any harm or injury that comes about from following
instructions or advice in this book.

Previously published as part of a larger volume, *Cook Smart*

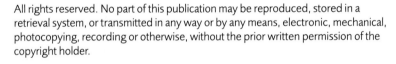

NOTES

Bracketed terms are intended for
American readers.

For all recipes, quantities are given in both
metric and imperial measures and, where
appropriate, in standard cups and spoons.
Follow one set, but not a mixture, because
they are not interchangeable.

Standard spoon and cup measures are
level.
1 tsp = 5ml, 1 tbsp = 15ml, 1 cup =
250ml/8fl oz.

Australian standard tablespoons are 20ml.
Australian readers should use 3 tsp in
place of 1 tbsp for measuring small
quantities of gelatine, flour, salt, etc.

American pints are 16fl oz/2 cups.
American readers should use 20fl oz/2.5
cups in place of 1 pint when measuring
liquids.

Electric oven temperatures in this book are
for conventional ovens. When using a fan
oven, the temperature will probably need
to be reduced by about

10–20°C/20–40°F. Since ovens vary, you
should check with your manufacturer's
instruction book for guidance.

The nutritional analysis given for each
recipe is calculated per portion (i.e. serving
or item), unless otherwise stated. If the
recipe gives a range, such as Serves 4–6,
then the nutritional analysis will be for
the smaller portion size, i.e. 6 servings.
Measurements for sodium do not include
salt added to taste.

Medium (US large) eggs are used unless
otherwise stated.

Main front cover image shows Cod and
Bean Stew – for recipe, see page 45.

Contents

The Principles of Budget Cooking

Budget cooking is the notion of buying and using ingredients that will enable you to create a fabulous feast for less than it would cost to buy an ordinary sandwich from a store. Whatever your skill level or culinary preferences, with just a little common sense and planning you can produce a healthy, hearty and tasty two-course meal, complete with side dishes and accompaniments, for any occasion – from simple family suppers to dinner parties, barbecues and buffets.

About this book

Feeding a hungry family can be an expensive business, and with today's hectic lifestyle it is all too easy to disregard the importance of fresh, healthy home-made food. Lack of planning can result in huge amounts of food being thrown away, wasting both money and resources. However, with just a little bit of thought, some simple shopping tips and a wealth of inspiring recipes, you can create delicious meals without breaking the bank.

This book contains everything you need to know about what, when and where to buy the best value, best quality ingredients, and how to turn them into a wide range of healthy and delicious home-cooked meals. Detailed guidance on planning and preparation is given, covering everything from drawing up a weekly menu and managing a budget to shopping tips and buying in bulk. Many inspiring ideas for converting left-overs into delicious dishes make ingredients stretch further and will enable you to enjoy seasonal ingredients all year round.

Above: *Buying fresh produce to cook at home is not only cheaper than using ready-made meals, but it is also likely to be much healthier and taste better.*

Expert advice on growing your own herbs both outside an inside the house is provided, as well as tips and techniques for easy ways to introduce flavour and texture to dishes using a range of herbs, spices and aromatics.

Storecupboard staples – ranging from baking basics such as flour and sugar to stock (bouillon) cubes, oils and aromatics – are listed in a comprehensive directory, and arm the budget cook with the power to convert simple ingredients into stunning meals. Sample menus make planning meals for different occasions easy and provide the inspiration for you to create your own menus.

How recipes are costed

The cost of each recipe is based on average prices of ingredients at large supermarkets, and assumes the use of goods that are middle of the range rather than at either end of the price scale. Unless otherwise specified, all fruit, vegetables, dairy, fish and meat are fresh rather than canned or frozen, and all eggs are free-range.

Above: *A well-stocked storecupboard can save you time and money when cooking, and will encourage you to try your hand at more home baking.*

Fresh ingredients are priced when they are in season, and it is important that you bear in mind that the price of these foods may rise, and their availability may be limited, when they are out of season.

Many items may be cheaper to buy at wholesalers, markets or independent stores – such as butchers, fishmongers and greengrocers – and special offers and bulk-buying will also bring the cost of ingredients down: shopping around is vital.

Items that appear under the "From the storecupboard" heading in the ingredients list in recipes are not included in the final cost, since they should all be part of the budget cook's storecupboard.

Suggestions for side dishes and accompaniments are provided in the introductions to the recipes to enable you to create healthy, balanced meals. Cook's tips and variations provide further information about ingredients and techniques and provide invaluable ideas for alternative flavours and textures.

Below: *Choosing good-quality ingredients will help you to create delicious dishes with the minimum effort and cost.*

How to use the key

Each recipe has been placed into one of three categories, depending on the overall cost of the dish per person. These categories are clearly illustrated by the symbols that appear beside each recipe name.

The categories are:

✳	Bargain
✳ ✳	Very economical
✳ ✳ ✳	Economical

These price bands are a guide to the relative cost of each recipe, with one star representing the cheapest dishes and three stars denoting those that are slightly more expensive. All you have to do is work out how much you want to spend, which courses you want to serve, and then simply combine recipes to create your perfect meal. Alternatively you could use one of the menu plans provided.

Preparation and Planning

Proper prior planning helps to ensure that you eat a wide variety of foods and make the most of seasonal produce. If you know that you are going to be short of time in the evenings, then you should consider preparing make-ahead meals and stocking up the freezer, so that you avoid the temptation to buy an expensive store-bought meal or unhealthy fast foods.

Weekly planning

For many people, the thought of planning an evening meal simply never crosses their minds until dinner-time arrives. This lack of forethought often results in people eating out or buying ready meals, both of which can be very costly if indulged in on a regular basis. A little bit of planning not only saves money, but it also ensures greater variety in the diet and can save time at the end of a busy day.

Nutritional guidelines indicate that the main meal each day should include a balance of protein, carbohydrates and several portions of vegetables, which help us on our way to the recommended 5-a-day target. Planning a weekly menu ensures that this balance of food groups is covered every day, makes shopping easier, and gives us greater control over the variety of foods eaten. It also helps to prevent waste, as you can plan how and when to use fresh ingredients, ensuring that if necessary they are either eaten shortly after they are bought, or that they are incorporated into dishes that are then frozen.

The easiest way to plan a weekly menu is to fill in a simple chart that you create yourself at home. This shows at a glance which courses and dishes are going to be served, and makes sticking to a budget much easier. All the family can be involved in this planning process, making everyone feel that their food preferences are being acknowledged and that they are taking an active role in deciding what they eat. Below is a sample weekly menu planner with some ideas for different combinations of courses and dishes:

Left: *Writing a list of exactly what meals you plan to make and the ingredients that you need to buy is an excellent way to ensure that you don't go over budget.*

Day of the week	Appetizer	Main dish	Accompaniment	Dessert
Monday		Chunky Tomato Soup with Noodles	Warm Crusty Bread	Hot Chocolate Pudding with Rum Custard
Tuesday	Mushrooms with Garlic	Mixed Bean and Aubergine Tagine with Mint Yogurt	Couscous or Boiled Brown Rice	
Wednesday		Dublin Coddle	Radicchio and Chicory Gratin	Oranges in Syrup
Thursday	Mushroom Caviar	Stir-fried Chicken with Thai Basil	Boiled Rice	
Friday		Cod and Bean Stew	Warm Crusty Bread	Meringue Layer Cake
Saturday	Crab, Coconut, Chilli and Coriander Soup	Gado Gado Salad		
Sunday		Chicken and Preserved Lemon Tagine	Boiled Rice	Autumn Pudding

Above: *Strip the tender roasted flesh from the carcass of a roast chicken and use the meat to make a casserole, pie or curry and the bones to make chicken stock.*

How to make the most of leftovers

Left-over food accounts for a large proportion of the food that is wasted every day. But this senseless waste is completely unnecessary, as left-over food can easily be transformed into a wide range of delicious new dishes. As part of the planning process you should take left-overs into account, and even make more than you need for one meal so that the leftovers can be converted into something else. Here are some budget-friendly ideas for ways in which you can make the most of the food you buy:

- A surprising amount of flesh can be stripped from a carcass after a roast meal, and this delicious cooked meat can be converted into a wide range of pies, curries, soups or even simply fried with onions to create a tasty and very quick supper. The stripped carcass can then be converted into home-made stock for use in any number of recipes. Left-over vegetables can be combined with the stock and flesh, if you like, to create a tasty soup, or fried up to make a variation on Bubble and Squeak.
- Cold roast beef, pork, chicken and turkey make excellent sandwich fillers, or can be served with a baked potato and salad for an easy supper dish.
- It is a good idea to make more Bolognese sauce than you actually need, as it freezes very well and forms the basis of many dishes, such as lasagne, moussaka, cottage pie and chilli con carne.
- The same applies for meat stews, which are easily made into pies with the addition of a potato or pastry topping.
- With the addition of a few ingredients, most left-over fish can be made into pies, tarts, salads or sandwich fillings, and the bones can be used to make fish stock.

- Boiled or steamed potatoes can be sliced and transformed into a Spanish omelette, or cubed and combined with corned beef, onions and tomato sauce.
- Other boiled or steamed vegetables make an almost instant ragu or curry when combined with a can of chopped tomatoes and a few storecupboard flavourings.
- Left-over pasta and rice is often thrown away because it is cheap. This is a waste, as it can be used to create a cold pasta salad, or to bulk out omelettes and soups.
- Cooked beans, peas and lentils can be readily incorporated into many meat and vegetable dishes, adding protein, texture and flavour as well as making more expensive ingredients stretch further.
- Cooked chickpeas can be puréed to make home-made hummus, and black beans are delicious when combined with chopped tomatoes, avocado, spring onions (scallions), coriander (cilantro) and lemon juice.
- Cold beans make a nutritious salad when combined with a little olive oil, lemon juice and seasoning.
- Stale bread has many uses: it can also be brushed with oil and grilled (broiled) or fried to make home-made croûtons, added to soups, dipped in egg and made into French toast, or used in recipes such as Autumn Pudding or Bread and Butter Pudding with Whiskey Sauce.
- Left-over stewed fruit makes a healthy and delicious topping for porridge (oatmeal), yogurt and ice cream, and can be added to fruit pies, cobblers and crumbles.
- You can use the hard rind from cheeses such as grano pedano to add flavour to soups and sauces. Simply add it at the start of cooking and remove before serving.
- Add left-over sauces and gravies to soups and pies, making sure that the flavours complement each other.

Above: *Making Autumn Pudding is an excellent way of converting a glut of fresh seasonal fruit and some stale bread into a truly stunning dessert.*

Shopping and Grow-your-own

Before you go shopping, you should have a list of the items you want to buy. This list not only ensures that you don't forget anything, but it also helps to prevent you from impulse buying and going over budget. Growing your own herbs at home ensures a cheap source of fresh ingredients are always at hand.

Above: *Greengrocers and markets often offer a better range of locally grown seasonal produce than supermarkets, so shop around to get the best value, variety and quality.*

Shopping around

The cost of produce varies from store to store, as well as from season to season, and it is important that you shop around to get the best deal and the best quality. Many of us get into the habit of visiting the same supermarket every week and don't explore other retailers. This is a bad habit to get in to, because while supermarkets are convenient and usually offer a good range of products all year round, other outlets such as farmer's markets, butchers, greengrocers and other independent shops may be cheaper, or stock a wider range of fresh seasonal or speciality ingredients.

Many stores have multi-buy offers, as well as bargain bins and reduced-to-clear items, and it is a good idea to find out when stores do their stock turn-over, as this is the time when they are most like to drastically reduce the cost of items in order to clear the stock. By finding out this information, you can pick up great bargains on a weekly basis and drastically reduce your overall shopping bill. It is important to note, however, that you should look at the quality of the produce that has been reduced, and only buy it if it is on your list and you are going to use it immediately or freeze it.

The internet is a very convenient way of doing the weekly shopping, and it can save you money as well as time. By buying online you can avoid the temptation to impulse buy, and by comparing the prices at different stores, you can ensure that you get the best deal. The drawback with internet shopping, however, is that you can't check the quality of the fresh produce, and although multi-buy deals apply, you usually can't get reduced-to-clear items. Smaller, independent retailers often have their own websites, too, and it is important to check both the price and range of produce that they offer, as well as delivery costs.

Specialist wholesale stores represent extremely good value for money if you are bulk-buying for a party or have the space to store large quantities of food. Some outlets require membership, which may only be granted to businesses, so it is worth checking this before travelling to the store. You should also check that there is not a minimum purchase requirement, or you may end up spending more than you budgeted for.

Getting the best deal

Buying in bulk, in conjunction with shopping around, is often the best way to reduce the relative cost of foods. It is, however, important to take several factors into consideration. If you are buying fresh produce, you will need to use it quickly, freeze it or preserve it as jams, pickles, chutneys or other long-lasting foodstuffs. If you are buying a large quantity of canned, bottled or packet goods, you will need space to store them, and you should be aware that they may have a limited shelf life.

Despite these factors, bulk-buying can save you money, as well as allowing you to stockpile seasonal produce so that it is available all year round. If you are short of space or have a small household, you could join forces with a friend or neighbour and split the cost and the produce. In this way you both benefit from the reduced cost but are not overwhelmed with more food than you can deal with.

Buying fresh produce when it is in season ensures that you get the best quality and value for your money. Almost all fresh food is most abundant at one particular time of the year, and it is a good idea to make the most of it when it is available. Eating seasonal meat, fish, fruit and vegetables also helps to ensure variety in your diet, and encourages experimentation in the kitchen.

Many supermarkets offer fresh produce all year round, whatever the season. It is worth considering that food that has been imported from abroad may have lost some of its taste and nutritional value, and may have been treated with preservatives. Imported food is also often more expensive than home-grown seasonal produce.

Picking your own fruit and vegetables, either from your own garden or from farms, is a fun way of gathering fresh produce. By taking children along to help, you will educate them about the food they eat as well as giving them a great day out in the fresh air. In rural areas you can often buy eggs directly from farms, which ensures that they are absolutely fresh, and they are often better value. Please note, you should always check that the eggs have both a use-by date and a mark to show that they have been produced to the highest standards of food safety. If in doubt, do not buy them.

Growing leafy herbs in containers

Most herbs grow well in containers, and there is a wide variety to choose from. A collection of containers of different shapes makes an attractive display on the patio. Do not choose anything too large if you want to be able to move pots around, for example, when you want to bring them into a sheltered position during the winter.

Above: *Growing herbs indoors is easy, and will fill your kitchen with their distinctive aroma.*

Above: *Take children along to pick-your-own farms or to harvest home-grown produce from the garden – it is fun, and it will help them to understand how food is produced.*

For convenience, several different herbs can be grown in one container, but bear in mind that they are not all compatible. Mint and parsley do not grow well together and fennel does not mix with caraway, dill or coriander (cilantro). Mint, tarragon and chives are best grown in separate containers as they will stifle any other herbs they are mixed with. Some herbs, such as rosemary, thyme, marjoram and sage like a sunny spot, while mint, chervil and chives prefer more filtered light.

During the spring and summer months all container-grown herbs need daily watering, as they can dry out in a matter of hours. However, do not be tempted to overwater any herbs. The soil should never become waterlogged. Whatever type of pot you choose, make sure there is a hole in the base for drainage. Fill the base with a layer of broken terracotta or stones and then a layer of grit or sand before filling with potting compost (soil mix). Once the herbs have been planted and watered, raise the container off the ground to free the drainage holes.

Growing herbs indoors

Most culinary herbs will thrive indoors provided they are sited in a light and sunny position and enjoy a fairly humid environment, away from central heating and severe temperature extremes. Indoor herbs benefit from being grown collectively because of the massed humidity. Basil is one of the most successful herbs to grow indoors as it is protected from garden pests which often decimate it outside. Care must be taken not to overuse indoor herbs, otherwise the plant will die from loss of foliage.

Fuss-free Flavour

You don't need to spend a fortune on expensive ingredients to make delicious family food. A whole range of simple herbs, spices and aromatics can be used to complement and bring out the flavours of the main ingredient of the dish, without the need for lots of costly extra ingredients. Match the seasoning to the ingredient and try some of the simple techniques outlined below, which include stuffing, dry rubbing, marinating, glazing and infusing.

Flavours for fish

Classic aromatics used for flavouring fish and shellfish include lemon, lime, parsley, dill, fennel and bay leaves. These all have a fresh, intense quality that complements the delicate taste.

- To flavour whole fish, such as trout or mackerel, stuff a few lemon slices and some fresh parsley or basil into the body cavity before cooking. Season, then wrap the fish in foil or baking parchment, ensuring the packet is well sealed. Place the fish in an ovenproof dish or on a baking tray and bake until cooked through.

- To marinate chunky fillets of fish, such as cod or salmon, arrange the fish fillets in a dish in a single layer. Drizzle with olive oil, then sprinkle over crushed garlic and grated lime rind and squeeze over the lime juice. Cover and leave to marinate in the refrigerator for at least 30 minutes. Grill (broil) lightly until just cooked through.

- To make a delicious marinade for salmon, arrange the fillets in a single layer in an ovenproof dish. Drizzle with a little light olive oil and add a split vanilla pod. Cover and marinate for a couple of hours or overnight, if you have time. Remove the dish from the refrigerator, cover with foil and bake in the oven until cooked through. Remove the vanilla pod before serving.

Pepping up meat and poultry

Dry rubs, marinades and sticky glazes are all perfect ways to introduce flavour into meat and poultry. Marinating the tougher cuts of meat, such as stewing steak, also helps to tenderize it.

- To make a fragrant Cajun spice rub for pork chops, steaks and chicken, mix together 5ml/1 tsp each of dried thyme, dried oregano, finely crushed black peppercorns, salt, crushed cumin seeds and hot paprika. Rub the Cajun spice mix into the raw meat or poultry, then cook over a barbecue or bake until cooked through.

- To marinate red meat, such as beef, lamb or venison, prepare a mixture of two-thirds red wine to one-third olive oil in a shallow non-metallic dish. Stir in some chopped garlic and bruised fresh rosemary sprigs. Add the meat and turn to coat it in the marinade. Cover and chill for at least 2 hours or overnight before cooking.

- To make a mild-spiced sticky mustard glaze for chicken, pork or red meat, mix 45ml/3 tbsp each of Dijon mustard, clear honey and demerara (raw) sugar, 2.5ml/$\frac{1}{2}$ tsp chilli powder, 1.5ml/$\frac{1}{4}$ tsp ground cloves, and salt and ground black pepper. Cook over the barbecue or under the grill (broiler) and brush with the glaze about 10 minutes before the end of cooking time.

Vibrant vegetables

Most fresh vegetables have a subtle flavour that needs to be enhanced. When using delicate cooking methods such as steaming and stir-frying, go for light flavourings that will enhance the taste of the vegetables. When using more robust cooking methods, such as roasting, choose richer flavours such as garlic and spices.

• To add a rich flavour to stir-fried vegetables, add a splash of sesame oil just before the end of cooking time. (Do not use more than about 5ml/1 tsp, because it has a very strong flavour and can be overpowering.)

• To make fragrant, Asian-style steamed vegetables, bruise a couple of lemon grass stalks with a mortar and add to the steaming water, then cook vegetables such as pak choi (bok choy) over the water until just tender. Alternatively add a few kaffir lime leaves to the water. You could also place the aromatics in the steamer under the vegetables and steam as before until just tender.

• To enhance the taste of naturally sweet vegetables, such as parsnips and carrots, try glazing them with honey and mustard before roasting. Simply mix together 30ml/ 2 tbsp wholegrain mustard and 45ml/ 3 tbsp clear honey in a small bowl, and season with salt and ground black pepper to taste. Brush the glaze over the prepared vegetables to coat completely, then roast until they are sweet and tender. You could also use maple syrup and/or omit the mustard, if you prefer.

Fragrant rice and grains

Accompaniments to main course dishes, such as rice and couscous, can be enhanced by the addition of simple flavourings. Adding herbs, spices and aromatics can help to perk up the rice and grains' subtle flavour as well as adding a splash of colour. Choose flavourings that will complement the dish that the rice or grains will be served with.

• To make fragrant rice to serve with Asian-style stir-fries and braised dishes, add a whole star anise or a few cardamom pods to a pan of rice before cooking. The rice will absorb the flavour during cooking.

• To make zesty herb rice or couscous, heat a little chopped fresh tarragon and grated lemon rind in olive oil or melted butter until warm, then drizzle the flavoured oil and herbs over freshly cooked rice or couscous.

• To make simple herb rice or couscous, fork plenty of chopped fresh parsley and chives through the cooked grains and drizzle over a little oil just before serving.

Making a bouquet garni

This classic flavouring for stews, casseroles and soups is very easy to make. Using a piece of string, tie together a fresh bay leaf and a sprig each of parsley and thyme. Alternatively, tie the herbs in a square of muslin (cheesecloth). It can be added to dishes at the start of the cooking time, left to impart its flavour for the duration, and then removed before serving.

Storecupboard Staples

A well-stocked storecupboard (pantry) is a must for the clever cook, and will help you to create delicious, economical dishes without the need for expensive ingredients or having to make a special trip to the supermarket. Staples range from flour, sugar, canned goods and oil to rice, pasta, dried herbs and stock (bouillon) cubes, and the following items have not been included when costing the recipes.

Above (clockwise from top): *Strong bread flour, self-raising flour, plain flour, and gluten-free flour.*

Flours

This is an essential ingredient in every kitchen. There are many different types, which serve many purposes in both sweet and savoury cooking – from baking cakes to thickening gravy and making cheese sauce.

Cornflour/cornstarch This very fine white flour is useful for thickening sauces and stabilizing egg mixtures, such as custard, to prevent them curdling.

Gluten-free flours For those with an allergy to gluten, which is found in wheat and other grains, gluten-free flour is an invaluable ingredient. It is widely available from most large supermarkets and health-food stores.

Wheat flours Plain (all-purpose) flour can be used in most recipes. Self-raising (self-rising) flour has a raising agent added and is useful for baking recipes. Wholemeal flour is available as plain (all-purpose) or self-raising (self-rising). Strong bread flour contains more gluten than plain flour, making it more suitable for making breads.

Raising agents You can add baking powder to plain flour to give a light texture to cakes and cookies. The powder reacts with liquids and heat during cooking and produces carbon-dioxide bubbles, which make the mixture rise.

Sugars

Refined and raw sugars can be used to sweeten and flavour many different types of dish, including cakes, bakes, pastries, cookies and desserts.

Brown sugars These dark, unrefined sugars have a rich, caramel flavour. There are several different types of brown sugar, including light and dark muscovado (brown) sugar and dark brown molasses sugar. As a general rule of thumb, the darker the sugar, the more intense its flavour. Always check that you are buying unrefined sugar, because "brown" sugars are often actually dyed white sugar.

Caster/superfine sugar This fine-grained white sugar is most frequently used in baking. Its fine texture is particularly well suited to making cakes and cookies.

Demerara/raw sugar This golden sugar consists of large crystals with a rich, slightly honeyish flavour. It is great for adding a crunchy texture to cookies.

Granulated sugar This refined white sugar has large crystals. It is used for sweetening drinks, and in everyday cooking; it can also be used as a crunchy cookie or cake topping, or stirred into crumble mixtures for extra texture.

Icing/confectioners' sugar The finest of all the refined sugars, this sugar has a powdery texture. It is used for making icing and sweetening flavoured creams. It is also excellent for dusting on cakes, desserts and cookies as a simple yet effective decoration.

Right: *Granulated sugar has larger crystals than caster sugar but both are good for making cakes and desserts.*

Pasta and noodles

These are invaluable storecupboard ingredients that can be used as the base of many hot and cold dishes.

Pasta Dried pasta keeps for months in an airtight container – check the packet for information on its keeping quality. There is a wide variety of pasta in all shapes and sizes. Egg pasta is enriched with egg yolks. It has a richer flavour than plain pasta and is often more expensive than dried varieties, which are very cheap. Generally, the choice depends on personal taste – use whichever type you have in the cupboard. Cook pasta at a rolling boil in plenty of water. Fresh pasta cooks very quickly and is available chilled. It can be stored in the refrigerator for several days, or in the freezer for several months.

Egg noodles Made from wheat flour and eggs, these may be thick, medium or thin. Use them for stir-fries or as a cheap accompaniment to Chinese and Asian dishes.

Rice noodles These transluscent white noodles are a good alternative to wheat noodles – particularly for those on a gluten-free diet. They are available as broad flat or thin noodles that can be added to stir-fries and soups as well as used cold as a base for salads. Rice noodles are easy to prepare, because they don't need to be cooked. Simply soak in boiling water for about 5 minutes, then stir-fry, add to soups or toss with salad ingredients.

Below: *Tiny soup pasta is available in hundreds of different shapes – buy whichever shape you prefer, and use to make substantial soups that can be eaten for lunch, or as a light meal when served with bread.*

Above: *Egg noodles have a nutty taste and are extremely good value for money, as well as being very versatile. They can be served hot in Asian-style stir-fries and soups, and cold in salads.*

Couscous and polenta

Like pasta and noodles, couscous and polenta are very cheap and can be served as an accompaniment or act as the base of many dishes. They have a mild flavour, and go particularly well with other, strongly flavoured ingredients, such as aromatics, herbs and spices.

Couscous Made from durum wheat, couscous is often regarded as a type of pasta. Traditional couscous needed long steaming before serving, but the majority of brands available in supermarkets today are "instant" and need only brief soaking in water. It is the classic accompaniment to Moroccan tagines, but also goes well with all kinds of meat, fish and vegetable stews. It makes an excellent base for salads and is very economical.

Polenta This is made from finely ground cornmeal. It is cooked with water and served either soft (rather like mashed potato) or left to set and then cut into pieces that can be grilled (broiled) or fried. Quick-cook and ready-made polenta are available in most supermarkets and can be made into simple, hearty dishes. It is best served with flavourful ingredients.

Above: *Canned beans are cheap and versatile and can be used in stews, healthy salads or tasty dips and pâtés.*

Rice
This great-value grain can be served as an accompaniment, or form the base of sweet and savoury dishes.

Basmati rice This long-grain rice is widely used in Indian cooking. It is aromatic and cooks to give separated, fluffy grains. Brown basmati rice is also available.

Long-grain rice The narrow grains of white rice cook to a light, fluffy texture and are generally served as an accompaniment to main dishes. They also make a perfect base for other dishes such as stir-fries and salads.

Risotto rice This rice has medium-length polished grains. The grains can absorb a great deal of liquid while still retaining their shape. There are several types of risotto rice, including the popular arborio and carnaroli. When cooking risotto rice, it is imperative to stir it regularly. Liquid or stock should be added periodically throughout cooking to prevent the rice sticking to the pan and burning, and spoiling the overall taste.

Short-grain rice There are several types of short, stubby, polished rice such as pudding rice and sushi rice. These usually have a high starch content and cook into tender grains that cling together and can be shaped easily.

Dried beans, lentils and peas
These staples are a fantastic resource for any cook and provide a very good low-fat source of protein. They are very good value, and can be used to help a meat dish go much further, thus reducing the overall cost.

Beans There are a wide variety of beans available in many stores, including red and white kidney beans, butter (lima) beans, haricot beans, flageolet beans and cannellini beans. To use, place the dried beans in a large bowl, cover with cold water and leave to soak overnight, then rinse under running water and drain. Kidney beans are poisonous unless they are properly cooked, so you need to boil the beans vigorously for 15 minutes, then change the water and simmer for about $1^3/_4$ hours until they are tender.

Lentils Red, green and brown lentils are all extremely versatile and do not require pre-soaking. Simply rinse under cold running water and add to a wide range of dishes.

Chickpeas These peas have a lovely creamy texture and hearty taste and can be used to make home-made hummus or to bulk out soups, stews and salads.

Canned goods
Although many foods taste best when they are fresh, there are some canned foods which are as good as or better than the fresh variety. These include canned tomatoes, which are usually cheaper and much more convenient to use than fresh tomatoes; canned beans, peas and lentils, which simply require rinsing before use; and some canned fish and shellfish, such as tuna and crab, which are significantly cheaper than the fresh varieties and make excellent additions to baked pasta dishes and salads.

Below: *Brown basmati rice is both healthy and cheap.*

Left (from left to right): *Corn oil and vegetable oil are cheap and extremely versatile.*

Oils

Essential both for cooking and adding flavour, there are many different types of oil.

Corn oil Golden-coloured corn oil is inexpensive, has a strong flavour and can be used in most types of cooking.

Groundnut (peanut) oil This virtually flavourless oil is used for frying, baking and making dressings such as mayonnaise.

Olive oil Extra virgin olive oil is made from the first pressing of the olives. It has the best flavour but is the most expensive type, so it is best reserved for condiments or salad dressings. Ordinary olive oil is generally made from the third or fourth pressing of the olives, so it is cheaper and should be used for cooking.

Vegetable oil This is a blend of oils, usually including corn oil and other vegetable oils. It is cheap, flavourless and useful in most types of cooking.

Flavoured Oils

Herb-infused oil Half-fill a jar with washed and dried fresh herbs such as rosemary or basil. Pour over olive oil to cover, then seal the jar and place in a cool, dark place for 3 days. Strain the herb-flavoured oil into a clean jar or bottle and discard the herbs.

Chilli oil Add several dried chillies to a bottle of olive oil and leave to infuse for about 2 weeks before using. If the flavour is not sufficiently pronounced, leave for another week. The chillies can be left in the bottle and give a very decorative effect.

Garlic oil Add several whole garlic cloves to a bottle of olive oil and leave to infuse for about 2 weeks before using. If you like, you can strain the oil into a clean bottle and store in a cool, dark place.

Vinegars, sauces and condiments

Not only are vinegars, sauces and condiments perfect for serving with dishes at the table, they are also great for adding flavour and bite to simple dishes during cooking.

Vinegars It is worth buying a good-quality vinegar as it will keep better. White wine vinegar, cider vinegar, malt vinegar and balsamic vinegar are the most commonly used.

Soy sauce Made from fermented soy beans, soy sauce is salty and just a small amount adds a rich, rounded flavour to Asian-style stir-fries, glazes and sauces.

Tomato ketchup Add a splash of this strong table condiment to tomato sauces for a sweet-sour flavour.

Worcestershire sauce This brown, very spicy sauce brings a piquant flavour to casseroles, stews and soups.

Curry paste There are many ready-made curry pastes, including those for classic Indian and Thai curries. They can also be used to spice up burgers or meatballs.

Mustard Wholegrain mustard has a sweet taste and makes a mild salad dressing. French Dijon mustard has a piquant flavour which complements red meat. English mustard is excellent added to cheese dishes.

Passata/bottled strained tomatoes This Italian product, made of sieved tomatoes, has a fairly thin consistency and makes a good base for a tomato sauce.

Tomato purée/paste This concentrated purée is an essential in every storecupboard. It is great for adding flavour, and sometimes body, to sauces and stews.

Below: *Tomato purée (paste) can add extra flavour to tomato sauces, soups and stews of all types.*

Dried herbs and stock cubes

Cheap and very useful, dried herbs and stock (bouillon) cubes are convenient standbys when you don't have fresh herbs or stock to hand, although for some recipes you will only be able to use the fresh type. Dried herbs have a much more concentrated flavour than fresh, so be careful about how much you add or the flavour might be overpowering.

Basil This distinctive herb is the perfect partner to tomato-based dishes, and can be used in soups, stews and to make tomato sauces.

Bay Dried bay leaves are a perfectly satisfactory substitute for fresh bay leaves. They are used when making a bouquet garni and can be added to meat dishes, stews and casseroles before cooking. Remember to remove them from the dish before serving, as they are tough.

Oregano Dried oregano has a strong, pungent flavour that will permeate the whole dish, so use in moderation. It adds a distinctive aroma to Italian-style dishes, and is an integral part of a basic tomato sauce for spreading on pizzas or topping pasta dishes.

Rosemary This is another pungent herb that will enhance the flavour of many meat dishes, especially those made with lamb.

Below: *Store dried herbs, such as bay leaves, in airtight containers to help to preserve their flavour better.*

Above: *Rock or sea salt is generally regarded as the most superior type of salt available, and it is not treated with any chemicals. You will need to grind it in a mill or a mortar before adding to food.*

Sage Peppery-tasting sage has large, slightly furry leaves when fresh. Dried sage goes particularly well with pork, or in pasta sauces and in stuffings. It has a very strong flavour, so use in moderation or it will overpower the dish.

Tarragon This fragrant herb has a strong aniseed flavour, and is most often paired with fish and chicken dishes.

Stock (bouillon) cubes These handy cubes are an excellent way of adding flavour to a range of cooked meat and vegetable dishes, although if you are making soup, it is better to use home-made stock if you possibly can, because it is such a key ingredient and forms the basis of the dish. It is worth paying a little extra for good quality stock cubes because cheaper varieties tend to contain a lot of added salt and will give a less satisfactory result.

Salt

A key ingredient, salt can be used in moderation to add flavour and to bring out the taste of other foods. It also acts as a preservative when it is used in pickling and chutney-making, or when curing meats and fish, since it draws out the moisture and prevents decomposition. It is worth paying a little extra for rock or sea salt, since these types do not contain any added chemicals, which are often found in table salt. Sea salt has a stronger taste than table salt, so use it in moderation, and add a little at a time, tasting in between additions to prevent oversalting.

Spices

These flavourings play a very important role when cooking with relatively inexpensive ingredients, adding a warmth and roundness of flavour to simple dishes. It is difficult to have every spice to hand, but a few key spices will be enough to create culinary magic. Black pepper is an essential seasoning in every storecupboard; cumin seeds, coriander seeds, chilli flakes and turmeric are also good basics. Store spices in airtight containers in a cool, dark place. Buy small quantities that will be used up quickly, because flavours diminish with age.

Allspice This berry has a warm, slightly cinnamon-clove flavour. It is more readily available in its ground form and can be used in both savoury and sweet cooking.

Caraway seeds These small dark seeds have a fennel-like flavour and can be used in sweet and savoury dishes.

Cayenne pepper This fiery, piquant spice is made from dried hot red chillies, so use sparingly. It is excellent added to cheese dishes and creamy sauces and soups.

Chilli flakes Crushed dried red chillies can be added to, or sprinkled over, all kinds of dishes. You can easily make your own by drying fresh red chillies on a radiator and then crumbling them with your fingers.

Chinese five-spice powder This is a mixture of ground spices, including anise pepper, cassia, fennel seeds, star anise and cloves. It is a powerful mixture, so use sparingly.

Cinnamon This warm spice is available in sticks and ground into powder, and has many uses. Add sticks to Moroccan stews, and use powder in baking.

Cloves Available whole or ground, these dried flower buds are used in savoury and sweet dishes. Ground cloves are strong, so use sparingly.

Coriander Available whole or ground, this warm, aromatic spice is delicious with most meats, particularly lamb.

Cumin This warm, pungent spice works well with meats and a variety of vegetables.

Fennel seeds These little green seeds have a sweet, aniseed-like flavour that pairs well with chicken and fish.

Garam masala This mixture of ground roasted spices is made from cumin, coriander, cardamom and black pepper and is used in many Asian dishes. Ready-mixed garam masala is widely available, although the flavour is better when the spices are freshly roasted and ground.

Ginger The ground, dried spice is useful for baking. For a fresher flavour, it is best to use fresh root ginger.

Green cardamom The papery green pods enclose little black seeds that are easily scraped out and can be crushed.

Nutmeg This large aromatic seed is available in a ground form, but the flavour is better when it is freshly grated.

Paprika Used in many Spanish dishes, paprika is available in a mild and hot form. It has a slightly sweet flavour.

Pepper Black pepper is one of the most commonly used spices, and should always be freshly ground or it will lose its flavour. Green peppercorns have a mild flavour. They are available dried or preserved in brine. White pepper is hotter than green, but less aromatic than black.

Turmeric Made from dried turmeric root, the ground spice is bright yellow with a peppery, slightly earthy flavour and is used in many Indian dishes.

Vanilla Dried vanilla pods (beans) are long and black, encasing hundreds of tiny black seeds. Natural vanilla extract is distilled from vanilla pods and is a useful alternative to pods.

Above: *For the best flavour, grate whole nutmeg as and when you need the spice, using a special small grater.*

Sample Menus

Whether you are planning a lazy picnic, a family barbecue party or a Sunday lunch, you can provide an array of delicious dishes without blowing your budget. The key to success is to plan ahead – make sure that you know how many people are coming, if any of the guests have dietary requirements, and prepare ahead of time. These sample menus show what is possible, but you can easily adapt them.

Sunday Lunch

Sunday lunch is a great opportunity to gather friends and family together around the table to enjoy a delicious meal together. For a vegetarian alternative, why not try Roasted Aubergines with Feta Cheese and Fresh Coriander in place of meat?

Roasted Duckling with Potatoes ✳ ✳ ✳

Succulent, tender roast duck is always a hit, especially when it is served with a herb stuffing and lashings of home-made gravy.

Baked Winter Squash with Tomatoes ✳

The sweetness of the baked squash in this colourful dish perfectly complements the tender roasted duck and honeyed potatoes.

Bread and Butter Pudding with Whiskey Sauce ✳

Cheap and easy to make, this pudding is a great way to use up stale bread. Replace the sauce with custard, if you prefer.

Quick Mid-week Supper

After a busy day, the last thing you feel like doing is spending hours in the kitchen, so here is an example of a nutritious and easy meal that you can rustle up in next to no time at all.

Mushroom Caviar ✳

This tasty vegetarian caviar requires minimal preparation and makes a healthy and appealing appetizer.

Tortellini with Ham ✳ ✳

Pasta dishes are incredibly versatile, as well as being cheap and quick to prepare, making them ideal for a speedy supper.

Green Salad ✳

Use any combination of your favourite ingredients, such as lettuce, rocket (arugula), spring onions (scallions) and cucumber.

Family Barbecue

Simplicity and preparation are the key ingredients for a successful barbecue, so make sure that you have planned everything well in advance – and hope for good weather.

Chargrilled Chicken with Garlic and Peppers ✳ ✳ ✳
Simple yet delicious, chicken cooked on a barbecue is always popular. Here, chicken pieces are marinated in a spicy lemon and mustard sauce for several hours before being served with grilled tomatoes and lemon wedges.

Pitta Bread
Lightly toast pitta breads on the barbecue towards the end of the cooking time for the chicken. Alternatively, warm them through in the oven for a few minutes.

Oranges in Syrup ✳
This elegant orange dessert can be made ahead and left in the refrigerator until required. Serve on its own or with a spoonful of yogurt, cream or ice cream – perfect for a hot summer's day.

Picnic Hamper

The key to a glorious picnic is to make plenty of food that is both portable and easy to eat. It is a good idea to take paper plates and plenty of napkins, and to include an ice pack in the basket to keep everything cool.

Chicken Liver and Brandy Pâté ✳
Extremely cheap to make and greatly superior in flavour to bought versions, this home-made pâté is delicious spread on hunks of crusty bread or water biscuits (crackers).

Potato, Onion and Broad Bean Tortilla ✳ ✳
Slice this simple broad (fava) bean and potato tortilla into wedges or small pieces before packing into plastic containers. You can vary the ingredients according to the season – good alternatives include frozen peas, pieces of ham or grated Cheddar cheese.

Grilled Aubergine, Mint and Couscous Salad ✳ ✳
Chunks of tender aubergine (eggplant) are grilled with olive oil and then combined with flavoured couscous and mint in this effortless salad. It is delicious warm or cold, making it ideal for a picnic.

Fresh Fig Compote ✳ ✳ ✳
High in fibre and delicious to eat, fresh figs make an ideal light dessert when they are in season. Serve on their own or with spoonfuls of low-fat natural (plain) bio-yogurt.

Soups and Appetizers

ELEGANT, ECONOMICAL AND DELICIOUS, SOUPS AND
APPETIZERS ARE THE PERFECT WAY TO START ANY MEAL.
THIS CHAPTER CONTAINS A RANGE OF IRRESISTIBLE
CHOICES – INCLUDING HEARTY, WARMING SOUPS
THAT CAN BE SERVED WITH BREAD AS A MEAL IN
THEMSELVES, SUCH AS TUSCAN CANNELLINI BEAN
SOUP WITH CAVOLO NERO OR CRAB, COCONUT, CHILLI
AND CORIANDER SOUP – AS WELL AS EASY-TO-MAKE
CHICKEN LIVER AND BRANDY PÂTÉ, OR FINGER FOOD
LIKE POTATO, ONION AND BROAD BEAN TORTILLA.

Chunky Tomato Soup with Noodles ✳✳✳

This full-flavoured Moroccan soup is given a warming kick by the ras el hanout, a spicy paste that you can buy in most supermarkets.

SERVES FOUR

1 In a deep, heavy pan, heat the oil and add the cloves, onions, squash, celery and carrots. Fry until they begin to colour, then stir in the tomatoes and sugar. Cook the tomatoes until the water reduces and they begin to pulp.

2 Stir in the tomato purée, ras el hanout, turmeric and chopped coriander. Pour in the stock and bring to the boil. Reduce the heat and simmer for 30–40 minutes, until the vegetables are tender and the liquid has reduced a little.

3 To make a puréed soup, leave the liquid to cool slightly before processing in a food processor or blender, then pour back into the pan and add the pasta. Alternatively, to make a chunky soup, simply add the pasta to the unblended soup and cook for a further 8–10 minutes, or until the pasta is soft.

4 Season the soup to taste and ladle it into bowls. Spoon a swirl of yogurt into each one, garnish with the extra coriander and serve immediately.

2 onions, chopped

1 butternut squash, peeled, seeded and cut into small chunks

4 celery stalks, chopped

2 carrots, peeled and chopped

8 large, ripe tomatoes, skinned and roughly chopped

5–10ml/1–2 tsp store-bought ras el hanout

a big bunch of fresh coriander (cilantro), chopped (reserve a few sprigs for garnish)

60–75ml/4–5 tbsp creamy yogurt, to serve

FROM THE STORECUPBOARD

45–60ml/3–4 tbsp olive oil

3–4 cloves

5–10ml/1–2 tsp sugar

15ml/1 tbsp tomato purée (paste)

2.5ml/^{1}/$_2$ tsp ground turmeric

1.75 litres/3 pints/ 7^1/$_2$ cups vegetable stock

a handful dried egg noodles or capellini, broken into pieces

salt and ground black pepper, to taste

Energy 258kcal/1086kJ; Protein 7.6g; Carbohydrate 36.3g, of which sugars 18.3g; Fat 10.2g, of which saturates 1.7g; Cholesterol 0mg; Calcium 175mg; Fibre 6.9g; Sodium 72mg

Tuscan Cannellini Bean Soup with Cavolo Nero *

Cavolo nero is a very dark green cabbage with a nutty flavour that is available during the winter months. It is ideal for this Italian recipe, which is packed with flavour as well as being healthy and sustaining.

SERVES FOUR

250g/9oz cavolo nero leaves, or Savoy cabbage

FROM THE STORECUPBOARD

2 x 400g/14oz cans chopped tomatoes with herbs

400g/14oz can cannellini beans, drained and rinsed

60ml/4 tbsp extra virgin olive oil

salt and ground black pepper, to taste

1 Pour the tomatoes into a large pan and add a can of cold water. Season with salt and pepper to taste and bring to the boil, then reduce the heat to a simmer.

2 Roughly shred the cabbage leaves and add them to the pan. Partially cover the pan and simmer gently for about 15 minutes, or until the cabbage is tender.

3 Add the cannellini beans to the pan and warm through over a gentle heat for a few minutes.

4 Check and adjust the seasoning, then ladle the soup into bowls, drizzle each one with a little olive oil and serve.

Energy 227Kcal/950kJ; Protein 8.2g; Carbohydrate 22.3g, of which sugars 10.4g; Fat 12.2g, of which saturates 1.9g; Cholesterol 0mg; Calcium 60mg; Fibre 7.9g; Sodium 443mg

Smoked Mackerel and Tomato Soup ✳✳

All the ingredients for this unusual soup are cooked in a single pan, so it is not only quick and easy to prepare, but requires minimal clearing up.

SERVES FOUR

200g/7oz smoked mackerel fillets

4 tomatoes

1 lemon grass stalk, finely chopped

5cm/2in piece fresh galangal, finely diced

4 shallots, finely chopped

2 garlic cloves, finely chopped

45ml/3 tbsp thick tamarind juice, made by mixing tamarind paste with warm water

small bunch of fresh chives or spring onions (scallions), to garnish

FROM THE STORECUPBOARD

1 litre/1³/₄ pints/4 cups vegetable stock

2.5ml/¹/₂ tsp dried chilli flakes

15ml/1 tbsp Thai fish sauce

5ml/1 tsp light muscovado (brown) sugar

boiled noodles, to serve

1 Prepare the smoked mackerel fillets. Remove and discard the skin, if necessary, then chop the flesh into large pieces. Remove any stray bones with your fingers or a pair of tweezers.

2 Cut the tomatoes in half, squeeze out most of the seeds with your fingers, then finely dice the flesh with a sharp knife. Set aside until required.

3 Pour the stock into a large pan and add the lemon grass, galangal, shallots and garlic. Bring to the boil, reduce the heat and simmer for 15 minutes.

4 Add the fish, tomatoes, chilli flakes, fish sauce, muscovado sugar and tamarind juice. Simmer for 4–5 minutes, until the fish and tomatoes are heated through.

5 Serve immediately, garnished with chives or spring onions, with some plain boiled noodles for a more substantial meal.

VARIATION *For a spicier soup, you could use smoked peppered mackerel fillets. These are usually available in many large supermarkets, and add a delicious peppery flavour.*

Energy 203Kcal/845kJ; Protein 10.3g; Carbohydrate 5.3g, of which sugars 5g; Fat 15.8g, of which saturates 3.3g; Cholesterol 53mg; Calcium 21mg; Fibre 1.2g; Sodium 385mg

Crab, Coconut, Chilli and Coriander Soup ✳✳✳

Although fresh crab meat has a better flavour, you can use canned crab meat in this sensational soup to keep the cost down.

SERVES FOUR

1 Heat the olive oil in a pan over a low heat. Stir in the chopped onion and celery, and sauté gently for 5 minutes, until the onion is soft and translucent.

2 Add the garlic and chilli, mix to combine well, and cook for a further 2 minutes.

3 Add the tomato and half the coriander and increase the heat. Cook, stirring, for 3 minutes, then add the stock. Bring to the boil, then simmer for 5 minutes.

4 Stir the crab, coconut milk and palm oil into the pan and simmer over a very low heat for a further 5 minutes. The consistency should be thick, but not stew-like, so add some water if needed.

5 Stir in the lime juice and remaining coriander, then season with salt to taste. Serve in heated bowls with the chilli oil and lime wedges on the side.

1 onion, finely chopped

1 celery stick, chopped

2 garlic cloves, crushed

1 fresh red chilli, seeded and chopped

1 large tomato, peeled and chopped

45ml/3 tbsp chopped fresh coriander (cilantro)

500g/1¹⁄₄lb crab meat

250ml/8fl oz/1 cup coconut milk

30ml/2 tbsp palm oil

juice of 1 lime

hot chilli oil and lime wedges, to serve

FROM THE STORECUPBOARD

30ml/2 tbsp olive oil

1 litre/1³⁄₄ pints/4 cups fresh crab or fish stock

salt

Energy 228kcal/951kJ; Protein 23.6g; Carbohydrate 5.4g, of which sugars 5g; Fat 12.6g, of which saturates 3.7g; Cholesterol 90mg; Calcium 199mg; Fibre 1.1g; Sodium 767mg

Chicken Liver and Brandy Pâté ✳

This pâté really could not be simpler to make, and tastes so much better than anything you can buy ready-made in the supermarkets. Serve with crispy toast for an elegant appetizer.

SERVES FOUR

1 Heat the butter in a large frying pan until it is foamy. Add the chopped chicken livers and cook them over a medium heat for 3–4 minutes, or until they are browned and cooked through.

2 Add the brandy and allow it to bubble for a few minutes. Remove the pan from the heat, allow the mixture to cool slightly, then tip it into a food processor with the cream and some salt and pepper to taste.

3 Process the mixture until smooth and spoon into ramekin dishes. Level the surface and chill overnight to set.

4 Serve garnished with sprigs of parsley to add a little colour, and some lightly toasted bread.

50g/2oz/¹/₄ cup butter

350g/12oz chicken livers, trimmed and chopped

30ml/2 tbsp brandy

30ml/2 tbsp double (heavy) cream

toasted bread, to serve

FROM THE STORECUPBOARD

salt and ground black pepper, to taste

Energy 227kcal/942kJ; Protein 15.7g; Carbohydrate 0.2g, of which sugars 0.2g; Fat 16.3g, of which saturates 9.6g; Cholesterol 369mg; Calcium 13mg; Fibre 0g; Sodium 144mg

Mushroom Caviar ✳

The name caviar refers to the dark colour and texture of this dish of chopped mushrooms. Serve with toasted rye bread, and garnish with chopped hard-boiled egg, spring onion and parsley, if you like.

SERVES FOUR

1 Heat the oil in a large pan, add the chopped mushrooms, shallots and garlic, and cook gently for about 5 minutes, stirring occasionally, until browned.

2 Season the mixture with salt and pepper to taste, then continue cooking until the mushrooms give up their liquor.

3 Continue cooking, stirring frequently, until the liquor has evaporated and the mushrooms are brown and dry.

4 Leave the mixture to cool slightly, then scrape it in to a food processor or blender and process briefly until a chunky paste is formed.

5 Spoon the mushroom caviar into dishes and serve with plenty of toasted bread

450g/1lb mushrooms, coarsely chopped

5–10 shallots, chopped

4 garlic cloves, chopped

toasted bread, to serve

FROM THE STORECUPBOARD

45ml/3 tbsp vegetable oil

salt and ground black pepper, to taste

VARIATION *For wild mushroom caviar, soak 10–15g/¼–½oz dried porcini in about 120ml/ 4fl oz/½ cup water for about 30 minutes. Add the porcini and their soaking liquid to the browned mushrooms in step 2. Continue as in the recipe.*

Energy 116kcal/479kJ; Protein 2.9g; Carbohydrate 6.4g, of which sugars 4.4g; Fat 9g, of which saturates 1.3g; Cholesterol 0mg; Calcium 26mg; Fibre 2.3g; Sodium 8mg

Mushrooms with Garlic ✳

These spicy, garlic-flavoured mushrooms make an ideal vegetarian alternative for a dinner party or summer barbecue. .

SERVES FOUR

12 large field (portabello), brown cap (cremini) or oyster mushrooms, or a mixture of the three, halved

4 garlic cloves, coarsely chopped

6 coriander (cilantro) roots, coarsely chopped

FOR THE DIPPING SAUCE

1 garlic clove, crushed

1 small fresh red chilli, seeded and finely chopped

FROM THE STORECUPBOARD

30ml/2 tbsp sugar

90ml/6 tbsp rice vinegar

5ml/1 tsp salt

30ml/2 tbsp light soy sauce

ground black pepper, to taste

COOK'S TIP *If you like really spicy foods, do not remove the seeds from the red chilli.*

1 If using wooden skewers, soak eight of them in cold water for at least 30 minutes before making the kebabs. This will prevent them from burning over the barbecue or under the grill (broiler).

2 Make the dipping sauce by heating 15ml/1 tbsp of the sugar, rice vinegar and salt in a small pan, stirring occasionally until the sugar and salt have dissolved. Add the garlic and chilli, pour into a serving dish and keep warm.

3 Thread three mushroom halves on to each skewer. Lay the skewers side by side in a shallow dish.

4 In a mortar or spice grinder, pound or blend the garlic and coriander roots. Scrape into a bowl and mix with the remaining sugar, soy sauce and a little pepper.

5 Brush the soy sauce mixture over the mushrooms and leave to marinate for 15 minutes. Prepare the barbecue or preheat the grill, and cook the mushrooms for 2–3 minutes on each side. Serve with the dipping sauce.

Energy 78kcal/329kJ; Protein 5.8g; Carbohydrate 11.5g, of which sugars 9.1g; Fat 1.3g, of which saturates 0.3g; Cholesterol 0mg; Calcium 23mg; Fibre 3.3g; Sodium 1039mg

Potato, Onion and Broad Bean Tortilla ✳✳

The classic tortilla is simple to make and tastes fabulous. Serve it as a light summer lunch dish with a green leafy salad, or cut it into pieces, thread on to cocktail sticks (toothpicks) and serve as an appetizer.

SERVES SIX

1 Heat 30ml/2 tbsp of the oil in a deep 23cm/9in non-stick frying pan. Add the onions and potatoes and season with salt and pepper to taste. Stir to mix, then cover and cook gently, stirring, for 20–25 minutes.

2 Meanwhile, cook the beans in lightly salted, boiling water for 5 minutes. Drain well and set aside to cool. When the beans are cool enough to handle, peel off the grey outer skins. Add to the frying pan, together with the thyme or summer savory. Stir and cook for a further 2–3 minutes.

3 Beat the eggs with salt and pepper to taste and the mixed fresh herbs, then pour over the potatoes and onions and increase the heat slightly. Cook gently until the egg on the base sets and browns, gently pulling the omelette away from the sides of the pan and tilting it to allow the uncooked egg to run underneath.

4 Invert the tortilla on to a plate. Add the remaining oil to the pan and heat. Slip the tortilla back into the pan, uncooked side down, and cook for another 3–5 minutes. Slide the tortilla out on to a plate. Divide as you like, and serve warm rather than piping hot.

2 Spanish (Bermuda) onions, thinly sliced

300g/11oz waxy potatoes, cut into 1cm/$^1/_2$ in dice

250g/9oz/1$^3/_4$ cups shelled broad (fava) beans

5ml/1 tsp chopped fresh thyme or summer savory

6 large (US extra large) eggs

45ml/3 tbsp chopped mixed fresh chives and flat leaf parsley

FROM THE STORECUPBOARD

45ml/3 tbsp olive oil

salt and ground black pepper, to taste

Energy 673kcal/2812kJ; Protein 34.9g; Carbohydrate 59.2g, of which sugars 18.1g; Fat 35.2g, of which saturates 7.3g; Cholesterol 571mg; Calcium 272mg; Fibre 14.3g; Sodium 252mg

Pasta, Pulses and Grains

PASTA, BEANS, RICE AND NOODLES ARE LOW IN FAT, SUSTAINING AND EXTREMELY GOOD VALUE FOR MONEY. THEY ARE ALSO INCREDIBLY VERSATILE AND CAN BE USED TO CREATE WHOLESOME VEGETARIAN DISHES, SUCH AS ROSEMARY RISOTTO, INDIAN MEE GORENG, OR MIXED BEAN AND AUBERGINE TAGINE WITH MINT YOGURT. ALTERNATIVELY, BULK OUT MORE EXPENSIVE INGREDIENTS SUCH AS MEAT, AS IN TORTELLINI WITH HAM OR BOLOGNESE SAUCE, WHICH CAN BE USED IN MANY PASTA DISHES.

Tortellini with Ham ✳✳

This is a very easy recipe that can be made quickly from storecupboard ingredients. It is therefore ideal for an after-work supper.

SERVES FOUR

1 Cook the pasta according to the instructions on the packet. Meanwhile, heat the oil in a large pan, add the onion and cook over a low heat, stirring frequently, for about 5 minutes until softened. Add the ham and cook, stirring occasionally, until it darkens.

2 Add the passata to the pan. Stir well, then add salt and pepper to taste. Bring to the boil, lower the heat and simmer the sauce for a few minutes, stirring occasionally, until it has reduced slightly. Stir in the cream. Drain the pasta well and add it to the sauce.

3 Add a handful of grated grano padano to the pan. Stir to combine well and taste for seasoning. Serve in warmed bowls, topped with the remaining grano padano.

COOK'S TIP *Passata (bottled strained tomatoes) is handy for making quick sauces.*

250g/9oz meat-filled tortellini

¹/₄ large onion, finely chopped

115g/4oz cooked ham, diced

100ml/3¹/₂fl oz/scant ¹/₂ cup double (heavy) cream

about 90g/3¹/₂oz/generous 1 cup freshly grated grano padano cheese

FROM THE STORECUPBOARD

30ml/2 tbsp olive oil

150ml/¹/₄ pint/²/₃ cup passata (bottled strained tomatoes)

salt and ground black pepper, to taste

Bolognese Sauce ✳✳

This is a versatile meat sauce. You can toss it with freshly cooked pasta or, alternatively, you can layer it in a baked dish like lasagne.

SERVES FOUR

1 Heat the oil in a large pan, then add the chopped onion, carrot, celery and garlic and cook over a low heat, stirring frequently, for 5–7 minutes until softened.

2 Add the minced beef and cook for 5 minutes, stirring frequently and breaking up any lumps in the meat with a wooden spoon. Stir in the red wine and mix well.

3 Cook for 1–2 minutes, then add the passata, tomato purée, fresh parsley, dried oregano and 60ml/4 tbsp of the stock. Season with salt and pepper to taste. Stir well and bring the mixture to the boil.

4 Cover the pan, and cook gently for 30 minutes, stirring from time to time and adding more stock as necessary.

5 Taste for seasoning and toss with hot, freshly cooked pasta, or use in baked pasta dishes.

1 onion, finely chopped

1 small carrot, finely chopped

1 celery stick, finely chopped

2 garlic cloves, finely chopped

400g/14oz minced (ground) beef

120ml/4fl oz/¹/₂ cup red wine

15ml/1 tbsp chopped fresh flat leaf parsley

FROM THE STORECUPBOARD

45ml/3 tbsp olive oil

200ml/7fl oz/scant 1 cup passata (strained bottled tomatoes)

15ml/1 tbsp tomato purée (paste)

5ml/1 tsp dried oregano

about 350ml/12fl oz/1¹/₂ cups beef stock

salt and ground black pepper

Top: Energy 373kcal/1549kJ; Protein 17.4g; Carbohydrate 10.9g, of which sugars 3.5g; Fat 29.2g, of which saturates 14.8g; Cholesterol 79mg; Calcium 302mg; Fibre 1g; Sodium 1025mg

Above: Energy 340kcal/1410kJ; Protein 20.6g; Carbohydrate 4.3g, of which sugars 3.9g; Fat 24.5g, of which saturates 8.1g; Cholesterol 60mg; Calcium 27mg; Fibre 1g; Sodium 214mg

Indian Mee Goreng ✳✳

This is a truly international dish combining Indian, Chinese and Western ingredients. It is a delicious and nutritious treat for lunch or supper.

SERVES SIX

1 Bring a large pan of water to the boil, add the fresh or dried egg noodles and cook according to the packet instructions. Drain the noodles and immediately rinse them under cold water to halt cooking. Drain again and set aside.

2 Heat 30ml/2 tbsp of the oil in a large frying pan. Cut the tofu into cubes and cook until brown, then lift it out with a slotted spoon and set aside.

3 Beat the eggs with the water and seasoning. Add to the oil in the frying pan and cook without stirring until set. Flip over, cook the other side, then slide out of the pan, roll up and slice thinly.

4 Heat the remaining oil in a wok or large frying pan and cook the onion and garlic for 2–3 minutes. Add the drained noodles, soy sauce, ketchup and chilli sauce. Toss well over medium heat for 2 minutes, then add the diced potato.

5 Reserve a few spring onions to garnish, and stir the rest into the noodles with the chilli, if using, and the tofu.

6 Stir in the sliced omelette. Serve immediately on a hot plate, garnished with the remaining spring onion.

150g/5oz firm tofu

2 eggs

30ml/2 tbsp water

1 onion, sliced

1 garlic clove, crushed

1 large cooked potato, diced

4 spring onions (scallions), shredded

1–2 fresh green chillies, seeded and thinly sliced (optional)

FROM THE STORECUPBOARD

450g/1lb fresh or 225g/8oz dried egg noodles

60–90ml/4–6 tbsp vegetable oil

15ml/1 tbsp light soy sauce

30–45ml/2–3 tbsp tomato ketchup

15ml/1 tbsp chilli sauce (or to taste)

Energy 421kcal/1772kJ; Protein 13.7g; Carbohydrate 59g, of which sugars 4.2g; Fat 16.2g, of which saturates 3.2g; Cholesterol 85mg; Calcium 165mg; Fibre 2.7g; Sodium 416mg

½ cucumber, sliced lengthways, seeded and diced

4–6 spring onions (scallions)

a bunch of radishes, about 115g/4oz

225g/8oz mooli (daikon), peeled

115g/4oz/2 cups beansprouts, rinsed then left in iced water and drained

2 garlic cloves, crushed

45ml/3 tbsp toasted sesame paste

roasted peanuts or cashew nuts, to garnish

FROM THE STORECUPBOARD

225g/8oz dried egg noodles

60ml/4 tbsp groundnut (peanut) oil or sunflower oil

15ml/1 tbsp sesame oil

15ml/1 tbsp light soy sauce

5–10ml/1–2 tsp chilli sauce, to taste

15ml/1 tbsp rice vinegar

120ml/4fl oz/½ cup chicken stock or water

5ml/1 tsp sugar, or to taste

salt and ground black pepper, to taste

Sichuan Noodles ✳✳

This tasty vegetarian dish combines egg noodles with plenty of fresh vegetables in a rich, nutty sauce, with just a hint of chilli.

SERVES FOUR

1 Bring a large pan of water to the boil, add the noodles and cook according to the packet instruction. Drain and rinse them under cold water. Drain again and set aside.

2 Sprinkle the cucumber with salt, leave for 15 minutes, rinse well, then drain and pat dry on kitchen paper. Place in a large salad bowl.

3 Cut the spring onions into fine shreds. Cut the radishes in half and slice finely. Coarsely grate the mooli, using a mandolin or a food processor. Add all the vegetables to the cucumber and toss gently.

4 Heat half the oil in a wok or large frying pan and stir-fry the noodles for about 1 minute. Using a slotted spoon, transfer the noodles to a large serving bowl and keep warm.

5 Heat the remaining oil in the wok or frying pan and add the garlic to flavour the oil. Stir in the sesame paste, sesame oil, soy and chilli sauces, vinegar and chicken stock or water. Add a little sugar and season. Warm over a gentle heat.

6 Pour the sauce over the noodles and toss well. Garnish with peanuts or cashew nuts and serve with the vegetables.

Energy 499Kcal/2088kJ; Protein 11.8g; Carbohydrate 60.3g, of which sugars 7.1g; Fat 25g, of which saturates 5.3g; Cholesterol 23mg; Calcium 85mg; Fibre 4.5g; Sodium 510mg

Rosemary Risotto ✳✳

This is a classic risotto with a subtle and complex taste. It is very filling and quite rich, so it only requires a simple side salad as an accompaniment.

SERVES FOUR

1 onion, chopped

2 garlic cloves, crushed

175ml/6fl oz/^{3}/$_4$ cup dry white wine

60ml/4 tbsp mascarpone cheese

65g/2^1/$_2$oz/scant 1 cup freshly grated Parmesan cheese, plus extra, to serve (optional)

5ml/1 tsp chopped fresh rosemary

FROM THE STORECUPBOARD

400g/14oz can borlotti beans

30ml/2 tbsp olive oil

275g/10oz/1^1/$_2$ cups risotto rice

900ml–1 litre/ 1^1/$_2$–1^3/$_4$ pints/ 3^3/$_4$–4 cups simmering vegetable or chicken stock

salt and ground black pepper, to taste

1 Drain the beans, rinse under cold water and drain again. Purée about two-thirds of the beans fairly coarsely in a food processor or blender. Set the remaining beans aside.

2 Heat the oil in a large pan and gently fry the onion and garlic for 6–8 minutes until very soft. Add the rice and cook over a medium heat for a few minutes, stirring constantly, until the grains are thoroughly coated in oil and are slightly translucent.

3 Pour in the wine. Cook over a medium heat for 2–3 minutes, stirring all the time, until the wine has been absorbed. Add the stock a ladleful at a time, waiting for each quantity to be absorbed before adding more, and continuing to stir.

4 When the rice is three-quarters cooked, stir in the bean purée. Continue to cook, adding the remaining stock, until it is creamy and the rice is tender but still has a bit of "bite". Add the reserved beans, with the mascarpone, Parmesan and rosemary, then season to taste. Stir thoroughly, then cover and leave to stand for about 5 minutes. Serve with extra Parmesan.

COOK'S TIPS

• *Arborio rice is the best type of rice to use for making a risotto because it has shorter, fatter grains than other short grain rices, and a high starch content, which makes for a creamier risotto. By being coated in oil, the grains of rice absorb the liquid slowly and release their starch gradually, which helps to produce a creamy end result.*

• *You should use a large pan for making risotto, as it makes it easier to stir and allows the grains of rice to cook evenly and more quickly.*

Energy 531Kcal/2220kJ; Protein 20g; Carbohydrate 74.6g, of which sugars 5.2g; Fat 14g, of which saturates 5.6g; Cholesterol 23mg; Calcium 287mg; Fibre 6.4g; Sodium 569mg

Porcini Risotto ✳✳

This risotto is easy to make because you don't have to stand over it stirring constantly as it cooks, as you do with a traditional risotto. Serve with steamed green vegetables for a sustaining main meal.

SERVES FOUR

25g/1oz/¹/₂ cup dried porcini mushrooms

1 onion, finely chopped

FROM THE STORECUPBOARD

225g/8oz/generous 1 cup risotto rice

30ml/2 tbsp garlic-infused olive oil

salt and ground black pepper, to taste

1 Soak the mushrooms for 30 minutes in 750ml/1¹/₄ pints/ 3 cups boiling water. Drain through a sieve (strainer) lined with kitchen paper, reserving the soaking liquor. Rinse and pat dry.

2 Preheat the oven to 180°C/350°F/Gas 4. Heat the oil in a roasting pan on the hob (stovetop) and add the onion. Cook for 2–3 minutes, or until softened but not coloured.

3 Add the rice and stir for 2 minutes, then add the mushrooms. Mix in the mushroom liquor, then season, and cover with foil.

4 Bake in the oven for 30 minutes, stirring occasionally, until all the stock has been absorbed and the rice is tender. Divide between warm serving bowls and serve immediately.

Energy 258kcal/1074kJ; Protein 4.5g; Carbohydrate 46.1g, of which sugars 0.9g; Fat 5.8g, of which saturates 0.8g; Cholesterol 0mg; Calcium 15mg; Fibre 0.3g; Sodium 1mg

Mixed Bean and Aubergine Tagine with Mint Yogurt ✳✳

Beans are not only cheap, but they are also a very good source of protein. Here they are combined with aubergine (eggplant), fresh herbs, garlic and chillies to make a very healthy dish that is perfect for a cold winter's day.

SERVES FOUR

1 Place the soaked and drained kidney beans in a large pan of unsalted boiling water. Bring back to the boil and boil rapidly for 10 minutes, then drain.

2 Place the soaked and drained black-eyed or cannellini beans in a separate large pan of boiling unsalted water and boil rapidly for 10 minutes, then drain.

3 Place 600ml/1 pint/2^1/$_2$ cups of water in a large tagine or casserole, and add the bay leaves, celery and beans. Cover and place in an unheated oven.

4 Set the oven to 190°C/375°F/Gas 5. Cook for 1–1^1/$_2$ hours or until the beans are tender, then drain.

5 Heat 60ml/4 tbsp of the oil in a large frying pan or cast-iron tagine base. Pat the aubergine chunks dry, then add to the pan and cook, stirring, for 4–5 minutes. Remove and set aside.

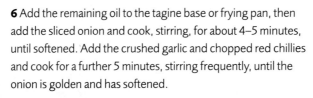

6 Add the remaining oil to the tagine base or frying pan, then add the sliced onion and cook, stirring, for about 4–5 minutes, until softened. Add the crushed garlic and chopped red chillies and cook for a further 5 minutes, stirring frequently, until the onion is golden and has softened.

7 Reset the oven temperature to 160°C/325°F/Gas 3. Add the tomato purée and paprika to the onion mixture and cook for 1–2 minutes. Add the tomatoes, aubergine, beans and stock, then season to taste.

8 Cover the tagine base with the lid or, if using a frying pan, transfer the contents to a clay tagine or casserole. Place in the oven and cook for 1 hour.

9 Meanwhile, mix together the yogurt, mint and spring onions. Just before serving, add the fresh mint, parsley and coriander to the tagine and lightly mix through the vegetables.

10 Garnish with fresh herb sprigs and serve immediately with the mint yogurt and some couscous or brown rice.

---

2 bay leaves

2 celery sticks, each cut into 4 matchsticks

1 aubergine (eggplant), about 350g/12oz, cut into chunks

1 onion, thinly sliced

3 garlic cloves, crushed

1–2 fresh red chillies, seeded and chopped

2 large tomatoes, roughly chopped

15ml/1 tbsp each chopped fresh mint, parsley and coriander (cilantro)

fresh herb sprigs, to garnish

FOR THE MINT YOGURT

150ml/^{1}/$_4$ pint/^{2}/$_3$ cup natural (plain) yogurt

30ml/2 tbsp chopped fresh mint

2 spring onions (scallions), chopped

FROM THE STORECUPBOARD

115g/4oz/generous ^{1}/$_2$ cup dried red kidney beans, soaked overnight in cold water and drained

115g/4oz/generous ^{1}/$_2$ cup dried black-eyed beans (peas) or cannellini beans, soaked overnight in cold water and drained

75ml/5 tbsp olive oil

30ml/2 tbsp tomato purée (paste)

5ml/1 tsp paprika

300ml/^{1}/$_2$ pint/1^1/$_4$ cups vegetable stock

salt and ground black pepper, to taste

Energy 209Kcal/890kJ; Protein 16.6g; Carbohydrate 33.9g, of which sugars 9.4g; Fat 1.9g, of which saturates 0.5g; Cholesterol 1mg; Calcium 173mg; Fibre 12.3g; Sodium 62mg

Fabulous Fish and Shellfish

THE COST OF FISH AND SHELLFISH CAN VARY
TREMENDOUSLY DEPENDING ON WHERE YOU LIVE,
THE TYPE OF FISH, AND WHAT SEASON IT IS. OILY FISH,
SUCH AS SARDINES, FIRM-FLESHED WHITE FISH SUCH
AS HADDOCK, AND SHELLFISH SUCH AS SQUID ARE
ALL USUALLY GOOD VALUE FOR MONEY. SO WHY
NOT INDULGE YOURSELF WITHOUT BREAKING THE
BANK WITH DELICATE SMOKED HADDOCK FLAN,
SUPER-HEALTHY BARBECUED SARDINES WITH ORANGE
AND PARSLEY, OR SPICY SQUID STEW?

Hake with Lemon Sauce ✳✳✳

This healthy dish is perfect on its own as a light lunch, or can be served with steamed new potatoes for a more substantial main course.

SERVES FOUR

500g/1¼lb fresh spinach, trimmed of thick stalks

4 x 200g/7oz fresh hake steaks

175ml/6fl oz/³⁄₄ cup white wine

3–4 strips of pared lemon rind

FOR THE EGG AND LEMON SAUCE

2 large (US extra large) eggs, at room temperature

juice of ¹⁄₂ lemon

FROM THE STORECUPBOARD

30ml/2 tbsp plain (all-purpose flour)

75ml/5 tbsp olive oil

salt and ground black pepper, to taste

2.5ml/¹⁄₂ tsp cornflour (cornstarch)

1 Place the spinach leaves in a large pan with just the water that clings to the leaves after washing. Cover and cook over a medium heat for 5–7 minutes, then drain and set aside.

2 Dust the fish with the flour. Heat the oil in a large frying pan, add the fish and sauté gently for 2–3 minutes on each side. Pour in the wine, and add the lemon rind and some seasoning. Lower the heat and simmer gently for a few minutes, then add the spinach, and let it simmer for 3–4 minutes more. Remove from the heat.

3 To make the sauce, mix the cornflour to a paste with a little water. Beat the eggs in a bowl, then add the lemon juice and the cornflour mixture and beat until smooth. Gradually beat in a ladleful of the liquid from the fish pan, then beat for 1 minute. Add a second ladleful in the same way, and continue until all of the liquid is incorporated.

4 Pour the sauce over the fish and spinach, and return the pan to the hob. Allow to cook gently for 2–3 minutes, then serve immediately.

COOK'S TIP *Spinach can have a gritty texture if it is not washed properly. The best way to wash it is to swirl the leaves gently with your hand in a large bowl of cold water, then lift them out by hand into a colander positioned over a sink. Repeat the process until the water that drains from the colander runs clear.*

Energy 441Kcal/1,839kJ; Protein 43.6g; Carbohydrate 10.6g, of which sugars 2.3g; Fat 22.1g, of which saturates 3.5g; Cholesterol 141mg; Calcium 273mg; Fibre 2.9g; Sodium 413mg

1 large red (bell) pepper

4 rashers (strips) streaky (fatty) bacon, roughly chopped

4 garlic cloves, finely chopped

1 onion, sliced

5ml/1 tsp hot pimentón (smoked Spanish paprika)

large pinch of saffron threads or 1 sachet powdered saffron, soaked in 45ml/3 tbsp hot water

6 plum tomatoes, quartered

350g/12oz fresh skinned cod fillet, cut into large chunks

45ml/3 tbsp chopped fresh coriander (cilantro), plus a few sprigs to garnish

crusty bread, to serve

FROM THE STORECUPBOARD

45ml/3 tbsp olive oil

10ml/2 tsp paprika

400g/14oz can haricot (navy) beans, drained and rinsed

about 600ml/1 pint/ 2¹/₂ cups fish stock

salt and ground black pepper, to taste

> **COOK'S TIP**
> *Cod is a popular white fish despite having been over-fished. Ensure that you buy fish that comes from a carefully controlled source, or else use an alternative white fish, such as hoki, hake, haddock, whiting, coley or pollack.*

Cod and Bean Stew ✳✳

Everything is cooked in one pot in this divine dish, which combines fresh cod with luxurious saffron and smoked paprika-spiced beans.

SERVES EIGHT

1 Preheat the grill (broiler) and line the pan with foil. Halve the red pepper and scoop out the seeds. Place the halves, cut-side down, in the grill pan and grill (broil) under a hot heat for about 10–15 minutes, until the skin is charred.

2 Put the pepper into a plastic bag, seal and leave for 10 minutes to steam. Remove from the bag, peel off the skin and discard. Chop the pepper into large pieces.

3 Heat the oil in a pan, then add the bacon and garlic. Fry for 2 minutes, then add the onion. Cover and cook for 5 minutes until the onion is soft. Stir in the paprika and pimentón, the saffron and its soaking water, and salt and pepper to taste.

4 Stir in the beans and add just enough stock to cover. Bring to the boil and simmer, uncovered, for about 15 minutes, stirring to prevent sticking. Stir in the chopped pepper and tomato quarters. Drop in the cubes of cod and bury them in the sauce.

5 Cover and simmer for 5 minutes. Stir in the chopped coriander. Serve in warmed soup plates or bowls, garnished with the coriander sprigs. Eat with lots of crusty bread.

Energy 181kcal/757kJ; Protein 14.4g; Carbohydrate 13.4g, of which sugars 6g; Fat 8.1g, of which saturates 1.8g; Cholesterol 28mg; Calcium 59mg; Fibre 4.6g; Sodium 388mg

Smoked Haddock Flan ✳✳✳

The classic combination of potatoes and smoked fish is reworked in pastry. Always ask your fishmonger for "pale" smoked rather than "yellow" haddock as the latter tends to have been dyed to look bright and often has not been smoked properly at all. It is worth paying the extra for the real thing.

SERVES FOUR

1 Preheat the oven to 200°C/400°F/Gas 6. Use a food processor to make the pastry. Put the flour, salt and butter into the food processor bowl and process until the mixture resembles fine breadcrumbs. Pour in a little cold water (you will need about 40ml/8 tsp but see Cook's Tip) and continue to process until the mixture forms a ball. If this takes longer than 30 seconds add a dash or two more water.

2 Take the pastry ball out of the food processor, wrap it in clear film (plastic wrap) and leave it to rest in a cool place for about 30 minutes.

3 Roll out the pastry and use it to line a 20cm/8in flan tin (quiche pan). Prick the base of the pastry all over with a fork then bake blind in the preheated oven for 20 minutes.

4 Put the haddock fillets in a pan with the milk, peppercorns and thyme. Poach for 10 minutes. Remove the fish from the pan using a slotted spoon and flake the flesh into small chunks. Allow the poaching liquor to cool.

5 Whisk the cream and eggs together in a large bowl, then whisk in the cooled poaching liquid.

6 Arrange the flaked fish and diced potato in the base of the pastry case, and season to taste with black pepper. Pour the cream mixture over the top.

7 Put the flan in the oven and bake for 40 minutes, until lightly browned on top and set.

FOR THE PASTRY

115g/4oz/1¹/₂ cup cold butter, cut into chunks

cold water, to mix

FOR THE FILLING

2 pale smoked haddock fillets (approximately 200g/7oz)

600ml/1 pint/2¹/₂ cups full-fat (whole) milk

150ml/¹/₄ pint/²/₃ cup double (heavy) cream

2 eggs

200g/7oz potatoes, peeled and diced

FROM THE STORECUPBOARD

225g/8oz/2 cups plain (all-purpose) flour

pinch of salt

3–4 black peppercorns

sprig of fresh thyme

ground black pepper, to taste

COOK'S TIPS

• Different flours absorb water at different rates. A traditional rule of thumb is to use the same number of teaspoons of water as the number of ounces of flour, but some flours will require less water and others more, so it is a good idea to add the water gradually. If you add too much water, the pastry will become unworkable and you will need to add more flour.

• Make sure that you use undyed smoked haddock rather than bright yellow dyed variety. It is well worth spending the extra money, as the flavour will be noticeably better.

Energy 734kcal/3064kJ; Protein 23.8g; Carbohydrate 58.4g, of which sugars 8.2g; Fat 46.8g, of which saturates 27.9g; Cholesterol 225mg; Calcium 280mg; Fibre 2.3g; Sodium 636mg

Barbecued Sardines with Orange and Parsley ✳

Sardines are ideal for the barbecue – the meaty flesh holds together and the skin crisps nicely – but they are equally delicious cooked under a grill (broiler). Serve them with boiled potatoes and a green salad.

SERVES SIX

6 whole sardines, gutted

1 orange, sliced

a small bunch of fresh flat leaf parsley, chopped

FROM THE STORECUPBOARD

60ml/4 tbsp extra virgin olive oil

salt and ground black pepper, to taste

1 Arrange the sardines and orange slices in a single layer in a shallow, non-metallic dish. Sprinkle over the chopped parsley and season with salt and pepper, to taste.

2 Drizzle the oil over the sardines and orange slices and stir to coat. Cover with clear film (plastic wrap) and chill for 2 hours.

3 Meanwhile, prepare the barbecue or preheat the grill (broiler) to high. Remove the sardines and orange slices from the marinade and place them directly on to a grill rack.

4 Cook the fish over the barbecue or under the hot grill for 7–8 minutes on each side, until the fish are cooked through. Serve immediately.

Energy 156kcal/649kJ; Protein 13.1g; Carbohydrate 1.7g, of which sugars 1.7g; Fat 10.8g, of which saturates 2.3g; Cholesterol 0mg; Calcium 73mg; Fibre 0.3g; Sodium 72mg

Fish Curry with Shallots and Lemon Grass ✳✳✳

This is a thin fish curry made with salmon fillets. It has wonderfully strong, aromatic flavours, and it should ideally be served in small bowls with plenty of crusty bread or plain boiled rice.

SERVES FOUR

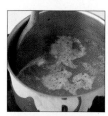

1 Place the salmon fillets in the freezer for about 30–40 minutes to firm up the flesh slightly. Remove and discard the skin, then use a sharp knife to cut the fish into 2.5cm/1in cubes, removing any stray bones as you do so.

2 Pour the vegetable stock into a pan and bring it slowly to the boil. Add the chopped shallots, garlic, ginger, lemon grass, dried chilli flakes, fish sauce and sugar. Bring back to the boil, stir well to ensure the ingredients are thoroughly mixed, then reduce the heat and simmer gently for about 15 minutes.

3 Add the fish pieces, bring back to the boil, then turn off the heat. Leave the curry to stand for 10–15 minutes, then serve in small bowls.

450g/1lb salmon fillets

4 shallots, finely chopped

2 garlic cloves, finely chopped

2.5cm/1in piece fresh root ginger, finely chopped

1 lemon grass stalk, finely chopped

2.5ml/$^1\!/_2$ tsp dried chilli flakes

FROM THE STORECUPBOARD

500ml/17fl oz/2$^1\!/_4$ cups vegetable stock

15ml/1 tbsp Thai fish sauce

5ml/1 tsp light muscovado (brown) sugar

Energy 218kcal/910kJ; Protein 23.4g; Carbohydrate 3.1g, of which sugars 2.7g; Fat 12.6g, of which saturates 2.2g; Cholesterol 56mg; Calcium 51mg; Fibre 0.8g; Sodium 322mg

Spicy Squid Stew ✳✳✳

This hearty stew is ideal on a cold evening, served with plenty of fresh crusty bread or steamed rice. The potatoes disintegrate to thicken and enrich the sauce, making a warming, comforting main course.

SERVES SIX

1 Clean the squid under cold water. Pull the tentacles away from the body. The squid's entrails will come out easily.

2 Remove the cartilage from inside the body cavity and discard it. Wash the body thoroughly.

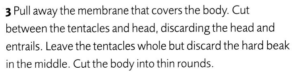

3 Pull away the membrane that covers the body. Cut between the tentacles and head, discarding the head and entrails. Leave the tentacles whole but discard the hard beak in the middle. Cut the body into thin rounds.

4 Heat the oil, add the garlic, chillies and celery and cook gently over a low heat for 5 minutes.

5 Stir in the potatoes, then add the wine and stock. Bring to the boil, then simmer, covered, for 25 minutes.

6 Remove from the heat and stir in the squid, tomatoes and parsley. Cover the pan and leave to stand until the squid is cooked. Serve immediately.

600g/1lb 6oz squid

5 garlic cloves, crushed

4 fresh jalapeño chillies, seeded and finely chopped

2 celery sticks, diced

500g/1¼lb small new potatoes scrubbed, scraped or peeled and quartered

400ml/14fl oz/1²/₃ cups dry white wine

4 tomatoes, diced

30ml/2 tbsp chopped fresh flat leaf parsley

white rice or arepas (corn breads), to serve

FROM THE STORECUPBOARD

45ml/3 tbsp olive oil

400ml/14fl oz/1²/₃ cups fish stock

salt

Energy 247kcal/1041kJ; Protein 17.6g; Carbohydrate 17.4g, of which sugars 3.8g; Fat 7.8g, of which saturates 1.3g; Cholesterol 225mg; Calcium 48mg; Fibre 2g; Sodium 136mg

Crab and Tofu Stir-fry ✳✳✳

For a year-round light meal, this stir-fry is a delicious choice. Use canned crab meat, as it is much more economical than fresh. Serve with fine egg noodles, if you like, as a special supper for two.

SERVES TWO

200g/7oz silken tofu

2 garlic cloves, finely chopped

115g/4oz canned crab meat

100g/3³/₄oz baby corn, halved lengthways

2 spring onions (scallions), chopped

1 fresh red chilli, seeded and finely chopped

juice of 1 lime

small bunch fresh coriander (cilantro), chopped, to garnish

lime wedges, to serve

FROM THE STORECUPBOARD

60ml/4 tbsp vegetable oil

30ml/2 tbsp soy sauce

15ml/1 tbsp Thai fish sauce

5ml/1 tsp light muscovado (brown) sugar

1 Drain the silken tofu, if necessary. Using a sharp knife, cut the tofu into 1cm/¹/₂in cubes.

2 Heat the oil in a wok or large, heavy frying pan. Add the tofu cubes and stir-fry until golden. Remove the tofu with a slotted spoon and set aside.

3 Add the garlic to the wok or pan and stir-fry for about 1 minute, or until golden. Add the crab meat, tofu, corn, spring onions, chilli, soy sauce, fish sauce and sugar. Cook, stirring constantly, until the vegetables are just tender.

4 Stir in the lime juice, sprinkle with coriander and serve in dishes with lime wedges, and fine egg noodles, if you like.

Energy 357kcal/1478kJ; Protein 21.5g; Carbohydrate 6.6g, of which sugars 5.6g; Fat 27.3g, of which saturates 3.2g; Cholesterol 41mg; Calcium 637mg; Fibre 2g; Sodium 2501mg

Perfect Poultry

THE SUCCULENT FLESH OF CHICKEN AND DUCK IS THE
PERFECT PARTNER FOR A WIDE RANGE OF DIVERSE
INGREDIENTS AND CAN BE COOKED IN MANY
DIFFERENT WAYS, MAKING IT BOTH ECONOMICAL AND
VERSATILE. RECIPES IN THIS CHAPTER RANGE FROM
QUICK-AND-EASY DISHES SUCH AS STIR-FRIED CHICKEN
WITH THAI BASIL OR CHARGRILLED CHICKEN WITH
GARLIC AND PEPPERS, TO SLOW-COOKED MEALS LIKE
ROASTED DUCKLING WITH POTATOES OR CHICKEN
AND PRESERVED LEMON TAGINE.

Stir-fried Chicken with Thai Basil ✳✳✳

Thai basil, sometimes called holy basil, has purple-tinged leaves and a more pronounced, slightly aniseedy flavour than the usual varieties. It is available in most Asian food stores but if you can't find any, use a handful of ordinary basil instead. Serve this fragrant stir-fry with plain steamed rice or boiled noodles and soy sauce on the side as a quick and easy supper dish.

SERVES SIX

1 Using a sharp knife, slice the chicken breast portions into strips. Halve the peppers, remove the seeds, then cut each piece of pepper into strips.

2 Heat the oil in a wok or large frying pan. Add the chicken and red peppers and stir-fry over a high heat for about 3 minutes, until the chicken is golden and cooked through. Season with salt and ground black pepper to taste.

3 Roughly tear up the basil leaves, add to the chicken and peppers and toss briefly to combine. Serve immediately with rice or noodles.

4 skinless chicken breast fillets

2 red (bell) peppers

1 bunch of fresh Thai basil

FROM THE STORECUPBOARD

30ml/2 tbsp garlic-infused olive oil

salt and ground black pepper, to taste

rice or noodles, to serve

Crème Fraîche and Coriander Chicken ✳✳

Boneless chicken thighs are usually better value for money than chicken breast fillets, and the meat has a stronger taste. There is no need to buy ready-skinned thighs, since it takes seconds to skin them yourself. Be generous with the coriander leaves, as they have a wonderful fragrant flavour, or use chopped parsley instead. Serve with creamy mashed potatoes or steamed rice, and steamed vegetables.

SERVES FOUR

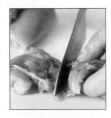

1 Remove the skin from the chicken thighs, then cut each into three or four pieces.

2 Heat the oil in a wok or large frying pan, add the chicken and cook for about 6 minutes, turning occasionally, until cooked through.

3 Add the crème fraîche to the pan and stir until melted, then allow to bubble for 1–2 minutes.

4 Add the chopped coriander to the chicken and stir to combine. Season with salt and ground black pepper to taste, and serve immediately with mashed potatoes or rice, and steamed seasonal green vegetables.

6 boneless chicken thighs

60ml/4 tbsp crème fraîche

1 small bunch of fresh coriander (cilantro), chopped

mashed potatoes or rice, and seasonal vegetables, to serve

FROM THE STORECUPBOARD

15ml/1 tbsp sunflower oil

salt and ground black pepper, to taste

Top: Energy 161kcal/675kJ; Protein 24.8g; Carbohydrate 4g, of which sugars 3.8g; Fat 5.1g, of which saturates 0.9g; Cholesterol 70mg; Calcium 26mg; Fibre 1.4g; Sodium 65mg

Above: Energy 222kcal/927kJ; Protein 26.8g; Carbohydrate 0.7g, of which sugars 0.6g; Fat 12.4g, of which saturates 5.4g; Cholesterol 148mg; Calcium 43mg; Fibre 0.6g; Sodium 120mg

Chargrilled Chicken with Garlic and Peppers ✳✳✳

An imaginative marinade can make all the difference to the sometimes bland flavour of chicken. This garlicky marinade, with mustard and chilli, gives tender chicken a real punch. Make sure the chicken has plenty of time to absorb the flavours before cooking.

SERVES SIX

1½ chickens, total weight about 2.25kg/5lb, jointed, or 12 chicken pieces

2 red or green (bell) peppers, quartered and seeded

5 ripe tomatoes, halved horizontally

lemon wedges, to serve

FOR THE MARINADE

juice of 1 large lemon

4 garlic cloves, crushed

2 fresh red or green chillies, seeded and chopped

FROM THE STORECUPBOARD

90ml/6 tbsp extra virgin olive oil

5ml/1 tsp French mustard

5ml/1 tsp dried oregano

salt and ground black pepper, to taste

1 Beat together the oil, lemon juice, garlic, chilli, mustard, oregano and seasoning in a large bowl. Add the chicken pieces and turn to coat thoroughly in the marinade. Cover with clear film (plastic wrap) and place in the refrigerator for 4–8 hours.

2 Prepare the barbecue or preheat a grill (broiler). When the barbecue or grill is hot, lift the chicken pieces out of the marinade and place them on the grill rack. Add the pepper pieces and the tomatoes to the marinade and set aside for 15 minutes. Grill the chicken pieces for 20–25 minutes.

3 Turn the chicken pieces over and cook for 20–25 minutes more. Meanwhile, thread the peppers on two metal skewers. Add them to the grill rack, with the tomatoes, for the last 15 minutes of cooking. Serve with the lemon wedges.

COOK'S TIP *If you are jointing the chicken yourself, divide the legs into two and make slits in the deepest part of the flesh. This will help the marinade to be absorbed more and let the chicken cook thoroughly.*

Energy 760Kcal/3,156kJ; Protein 61.7g; Carbohydrate 11.1g, of which sugars 10.8g; Fat 52.2g, of which saturates 13.3g; Cholesterol 313mg; Calcium 40mg; Fibre 3.1g; Sodium 235mg

Chicken and Preserved Lemon Tagine **

This fragrant Moroccan dish is perfect for a casual dinner party. Slowly cooked chicken pieces are served in an aromatic sauce, which melds the mellow flavour of the preserved lemons with the earthiness of the olives.

SERVES FOUR

1 onion, chopped

3 garlic cloves

1cm/¹/₂in fresh root ginger, peeled and grated,

pinch of saffron threads

4 chicken quarters, halved if liked

30ml/2 tbsp chopped fresh coriander (cilantro)

30ml/2 tbsp chopped fresh parsley

1 preserved lemon

115g/4oz/²/₃ cup Moroccan tan olives

lemon wedges and fresh coriander (cilantro) sprigs, to garnish

FROM THE STORECUPBOARD

30ml/2 tbsp olive oil

2.5–5ml/¹/₂–1 tsp ground cinnamon

750ml/1¹/₄ pints/3 cups chicken stock

salt and ground black pepper, to taste

1 Heat the oil in a large flameproof casserole and fry the onion for 6–8 minutes over a moderate heat until lightly golden.

2 Meanwhile, crush the garlic and blend with the ginger, cinnamon, saffron and a little salt and pepper. Stir into the pan and fry for 1 minute. Add the chicken in batches and fry over a medium heat for 2–3 minutes, until browned.

3 Add the stock, coriander and parsley, bring to the boil, then cover and simmer for 45 minutes, until the chicken is tender.

4 Rinse the preserved lemon, discard the flesh and cut the peel into small pieces. Stir into the pan with the olives and simmer for a further 15 minutes, until the chicken is very tender.

5 Transfer the chicken to a plate and keep warm. Bring the sauce to the boil and bubble for 3–4 minutes, until reduced and fairly thick. Pour the sauce over the chicken and serve, garnished with lemon wedges and coriander sprigs.

COOK'S TIP *The well-flavoured juice that is used to preserve the lemons can be used to flavour salad dressings or added to hot sauces.*

Spicy Chicken Casserole ✳✳

Serve this spicy take on classic chicken casserole with orzo, plain boiled rice, or thick-cut fried potatoes for a satisfying supper.

SERVES FOUR

1 Heat the oil in a large pan and brown the chicken pieces on all sides, ensuring that the skin is cooked and lifts away from the flesh slightly. Lift the chicken pieces out, set them aside on a plate, and keep them warm.

2 Add the chopped onion to the hot oil in the same pan and stir it over a medium heat until it becomes translucent.

3 Return the chicken pieces to the pan, pour over the wine and cook for 2–3 minutes, until it has reduced. Add the tomato purée mixture, cinnamon, allspice and bay leaves. Season well with salt and pepper.

4 Cover the pan and cook gently for 1 hour or until the chicken is tender. Serve with rice, orzo or fried potatoes.

1.6kg/3¹/₂lb chicken, jointed

1 large onion, peeled and roughly chopped

250ml/8fl oz/1 cup red wine

boiled rice, orzo or fried potatoes, to serve

FROM THE STORECUPBOARD

75ml/5 tbsp extra virgin olive oil

30ml/2 tbsp tomato purée (paste) diluted in 450ml/ ³/₄ pint/scant 2 cups hot water

1 cinnamon stick

3 or 4 whole allspice

2 bay leaves

salt and ground black pepper, to taste

Energy 767Kcal/3,195kJ; Protein 53.3g; Carbohydrate 32.5g, of which sugars 2.9g; Fat 47.7g, of which saturates 11.8g; Cholesterol 264mg; Calcium 51mg; Fibre 2.6g; Sodium 206mg

Roasted Duckling with Potatoes ✳✳✳

The rich flavour of duck combined with these sweetened potatoes glazed with honey makes an excellent treat for a dinner party or special occasion. Serve with steamed seasonal green vegetables.

SERVES FOUR

1 Preheat the oven to 200°C/400°F/ Gas 6. Place the duckling in a roasting pan. Prick the skin well. Combine the soy sauce and orange juice and pour over the duck. Cook for 20 minutes.

2 Place the potato chunks in a bowl, stir in the honey and toss to mix well. Remove the duckling from the oven and spoon the potatoes all around and under the duckling.

3 Roast for 35 minutes, then remove from the oven. Toss the potatoes in the juices and turn the duck over. Put back in the oven and cook for a further 30 minutes.

4 Remove the duckling from the oven and carefully scoop off the excess fat, leaving the juices behind. Sprinkle the sesame seeds over the potatoes, season and turn the duckling back over, breast side up, and cook for a further 10 minutes. Remove from the oven and keep warm.

5 Pour off the excess fat and simmer the juices on the hob (stovetop). Serve the juices with the duckling and vegetables.

**1 duckling,
giblets removed**

**150ml/¼ pint/⅔ cup
fresh orange juice**

**3 large floury potatoes,
cut into chunks**

30ml/2 tbsp clear honey

15ml/1 tbsp sesame seeds

**steamed seasonal greens,
to serve**

FROM THE STORECUPBOARD

**60ml/4 tbsp light
soy sauce**

**salt and ground
black pepper**

Energy 363kcal/1523kJ; Protein 23.3g; Carbohydrate 30.4g, of which sugars 11.8g; Fat 18.7g, of which saturates 4.9g; Cholesterol 108mg; Calcium 50mg; Fibre 1.6g; Sodium 198mg

Marvellous Meat

THERE IS A HUGE RANGE OF DIFFERENT TYPES
AND CUTS OF MEAT, ALL OF WHICH VARY IN PRICE AND
IN THEIR COOKING REQUIREMENTS. BY CHOOSING
GOOD-VALUE CUTS, COMBINING THEM WITH CHEAPER
INGREDIENTS AND COOKING IN AN APPROPRIATE
MANNER, MOST TYPES OF MEAT BECOME AFFORDABLE.
SO WHY NOT ADD A LITTLE SPICE TO YOUR LIFE WITH
MADRAS BEEF CURRY WITH SPICY RICE, OR TUCK INTO
A SUCCULENT LAMB AND CARROT CASSEROLE WITH
BARLEY FOR A HEARTY WINTER MEAL?

Madras Beef Curry with Spicy Rice ✳✳✳

Chillies are an indispensable ingredient of a hot and spicy Madras curry. After long, gentle simmering, they merge with the other flavourings to give a delectable result that goes perfectly with the spicy rice.

SERVES FOUR

1 Heat half the vegetable oil with half the butter in a large, shallow pan. When it is hot, fry the meat, in batches if necessary, until it is browned on all sides. Transfer to a plate and set aside.

2 Heat the remaining vegetable oil and butter and fry the onion for about 3–4 minutes until it is softened and lightly browned.

3 Add the cardamom pods and fry for 1 minute, then stir in the chillies, ginger and garlic, and fry for 2 minutes more.

4 Stir in the curry paste, 5ml/1 tsp each of ground cumin and coriander, then return the meat to the pan.

5 Stir in the stock. Season with salt, bring to the boil, then reduce the heat and simmer very gently for 1–1 1/2 hours, until the meat is tender.

6 When the curry is almost ready, prepare the spicy rice. Put the basmati in a bowl and pour over enough boiling water to cover.

7 Set aside for 10 minutes, then drain, rinse under cold water and drain again. The rice will still be uncooked but should have lost its brittle texture.

8 Heat the sunflower oil and butter in a flameproof casserole and fry the onion and garlic gently for 3–4 minutes until softened and lightly browned.

9 Stir in the remaining ground cumin and coriander, the green cardamom pods and the cinnamon stick. Fry for 1 minute, then add the diced peppers.

10 Add the rice, stirring well to coat the grains thoroughly in the spice mixture, and pour in the chicken stock.

11 Bring to the boil, then reduce the heat, cover the pan tightly and simmer for about 8–10 minutes, or until the rice is tender and the stock has been absorbed.

12 Spoon the spicy rice into a bowl and serve immediately with the curry. You can also serve this with a generous dollop of natural (plain) yogurt and some naan bread.

Ingredients

25g/1oz/2 tbsp butter

675g/1 1/2lb stewing beef, cut into bitesize cubes

1 onion, chopped

3 green cardamom pods

2 fresh green chillies, seeded and finely chopped

2.5cm/1in piece of fresh root ginger, grated

2 garlic cloves, crushed

15ml/1 tbsp Madras curry paste

FOR THE RICE

25g/1oz/2 tbsp butter

1 onion, finely chopped

1 garlic clove, crushed

4 green cardamom pods

1 small red (bell) pepper, seeded and diced

1 small green (bell) pepper, seeded and diced

FROM THE STORECUPBOARD

30ml/2 tbsp vegetable oil

10ml/2 tsp ground cumin

7.5ml/1 1/2 tsp ground coriander

150ml/1/4 pint/2/3 cup beef stock

salt

225g/8oz/generous 1 cup basmati rice

15ml/1 tbsp sunflower oil

1 cinnamon stick

300ml/1/2 pint/1 1/4 cups beef stock

Energy 717kcal/2984kJ; Protein 44.2g; Carbohydrate 53.8g, of which sugars 7.1g; Fat 36g, of which saturates 14.2g; Cholesterol 125mg; Calcium 41mg; Fibre 1.8g; Sodium 189mg

North African Lamb ✳✳✳

This dish is full of contrasting flavours that create a rich, spicy and fruity main course. For best results, use lamb that still retains some fat, as this will help keep the meat moist and succulent during roasting. Serve the lamb with couscous and steamed seasonal green vegetables.

SERVES FOUR

1 Preheat the oven to 200°C/400°F/Gas 6. Season the lamb with salt and pepper. Heat a frying pan, preferably non-stick, and cook the lamb on all sides until beginning to brown. Transfer to a roasting pan, reserving any fat in the frying pan.

2 Peel the onions and cut each into six wedges. Toss with the lamb and roast for about 30–40 minutes, until the lamb is cooked through and the onions are deep golden brown.

3 Tip the cooked lamb and onions back into the frying pan. Mix the harissa with 250ml/8fl oz/1 cup boiling water and add to the roasting pan. Scrape up any residue left in the in the pan and pour the mixture over the lamb and onions.

4 Stir in the prunes and heat until just simmering. Cover and simmer for 5 minutes, then serve with vegetables and couscous.

675g/1¹/₂lb lamb fillet or shoulder steaks, cut into chunky pieces

5 small onions

7.5ml/1¹/₂ tsp harissa

115g/4oz ready-to-eat pitted prunes, halved

seasonal green vegetables and couscous, to serve

FROM THE STORECUPBOARD

salt and ground black pepper, to taste

Energy 379kcal/1585kJ; Protein 35g; Carbohydrate 17.7g, of which sugars 15.4g; Fat 19.2g, of which saturates 8.8g; Cholesterol 128mg; Calcium 48mg; Fibre 3.1g; Sodium 151mg

Lamb and Carrot Casserole with Barley ✳✳

Barley and carrots make natural partners for lamb and mutton. In this convenient casserole the barley bulks out the meat and adds to the flavour and texture as well as thickening the sauce. The dish is comfort food at its best. Serve with boiled or baked potatoes and steamed green vegetables.

SERVES SIX

1 Trim the lamb of any fat or gristle and cut it into bitesize pieces. Heat the oil in a flameproof casserole, add the lamb and toss until the lamb is browned all over.

2 Add the vegetables to the casserole and fry them briefly with the meat. Add the barley and enough stock or water to cover, and season to taste.

3 Cover the casserole and simmer gently on the hob (stovetop) or cook in a slow oven, 150°C/300°F/Gas 2 for 1–1¹/₂ hours until the meat is tender.

4 Add extra stock or water during cooking if necessary. Serve immediately with potatoes and vegetables.

5 Alternatively, allow the casserole to cool, then refrigerate or freeze until needed. This will allow the flavours to mature. Thaw, if necessary, and reheat until piping hot before serving.

675g/1¹/₂lb stewing lamb

2 onions, sliced

675g/1¹/₂lb carrots, sliced

4–6 celery sticks, sliced

45ml/3 tbsp pearl barley, rinsed

baked or boiled potatoes and vegetables, to serve

FROM THE STORECUPBOARD

15ml/1 tbsp oil

stock or water

salt and ground black pepper, to taste

Energy 304Kcal/1263kJ; Protein 23.2g; Carbohydrate 13g, of which sugars 11.3g; Fat 18g, of which saturates 7.5g; Cholesterol 84mg; Calcium 53mg; Fibre 3.6g; Sodium 110mg

Roast Loin of Pork with Stuffing ✳✳✳

Sage and onion make a classic stuffing for roast pork, duck and turkey, with the sage counteracting the fattiness of the rich meats. Serve with apple sauce, roast potatoes and boiled or steamed vegetables.

SERVES EIGHT

1 Preheat the oven to 220°C/425°F/Gas 7. To make the stuffing, melt the butter in a pan and cook the bacon until it begins to brown, then add the onions and cook until softened. Mix with the breadcrumbs, sage, thyme, lemon rind and egg, then season.

2 Cut the rind off the pork in one piece and score it with a knife. Place the pork fat side down, and season. Add a layer of stuffing, then roll up and tie neatly. Lay the rind over the pork and rub in 5ml/1 tsp salt. Roast for 2–2¹/₂ hours, basting with the pork fat. Reduce the temperature to 190°C/375°F/Gas 5 after 20 minutes. Shape the remaining stuffing into balls and add to the pan for the last 30 minutes.

3 Remove the rind from the top of the pork. Increase the oven temperature to 220°C/425°F/Gas 7 and roast the rind for a further 25 minutes, until crisp. Mix the breadcrumbs and sage and press into the fat in the pan. Cook the pork for a further 10 minutes, then cover and set aside for 15–20 minutes.

4 Remove all but 30–45ml/2–3 tbsp of the fat from the roasting pan and place the pan on the hob (stovetop). Stir in the flour, followed by the cider and water. Bring to the boil, then simmer for 10 minutes. Strain into a clean pan, add the crab apple or redcurrant jelly, and cook for another 5 minutes.

5 Serve the pork cut into thick slices and the crisp crackling cut into strips with the cider gravy, garnished with thyme.

1.3–1.6kg/3–3¹/₂lb boneless loin of pork

60ml/4 tbsp fine, dry breadcrumbs

10ml/2 tsp chopped fresh sage

300ml/¹/₂ pint/1¹/₄ cups (hard) cider

150ml/¹/₄ pint/²/₃ cup water

5–10ml/1–2 tsp crab apple or redcurrant jelly

fresh thyme sprigs, to garnish

apple sauce, roast potatoes and vegetables, to serve

FOR THE STUFFING

25g/1oz/2 tbsp butter

50g/2oz bacon, chopped

2 large onions, finely chopped

75g/3oz/1¹/₂ cups fresh white breadcrumbs

30ml/2 tbsp chopped fresh sage

5ml/1 tsp chopped fresh thyme

10ml/2 tsp finely grated lemon rind

1 small (US medium) egg, beaten

FROM THE STORECUPBOARD

25ml/1¹/₂ tbsp plain (all-purpose) flour

salt and ground black pepper, to taste

Energy 446Kcal/1872kJ; Protein 53.6g; Carbohydrate 21.1g, of which sugars 5g; Fat 15.8g, of which saturates 6.1g; Cholesterol 161mg; Calcium 66mg; Fibre 1.2g; Sodium 356mg

Dublin Coddle ✳✳

This simple dish combines bacon and sausages, and is best accompanied by a crisp green vegetable, such as lightly cooked Brussels sprouts, purple sprouting broccoli or cabbage.

SERVES SIX

6 x 8mm/¹/₃in thick ham or dry-cured bacon slices

6 lean pork sausages

4 large onions, sliced

900g/2lb potatoes, peeled and sliced

90ml/6 tbsp chopped fresh parsley

green vegetables, to serve

FROM THE STORECUPBOARD

salt and ground black pepper, to taste

1 Cut the ham or bacon into chunks and cook with the sausages in a large pan containing 1.2 litres/2 pints/5 cups boiling water for 5 minutes. Drain, but reserve the cooking liquor.

2 Put the meat into a large pan with the sliced onions, potatoes and the parsley. Season, and add just enough of the reserved cooking liquor to cover completely.

3 Lay a piece of buttered foil or baking parchment on top of the mixture in the pan, then cover with a tight-fitting lid.

4 Simmer gently over a low heat for about 1 hour, or until the liquid is reduced by half and all the ingredients are cooked but not mushy.

5 Serve the coddle immediately with the Brussels sprouts or broccoli, or any other vegetable of your choice.

Energy 336kcal/1409kJ; Protein 12.7g; Carbohydrate 39.3g, of which sugars 9g; Fat 15.4g, of which saturates 6.2g; Cholesterol 33mg; Calcium 80mg; Fibre 3.6g; Sodium 695mg

Versatile
Vegetarian Dishes

VEGETARIAN DISHES ARE HEALTHY, ECONOMICAL AND
EXTREMELY ADAPTABLE, MAKING THEM AN IDEAL CHOICE
FOR FAMILY MEALS. FROM COLOURFUL, SUSTAINING
SLOW-COOKED DISHES SUCH AS VEGETABLE HOT-POT
OR HOT AND SPICY PARSNIPS WITH CHICKPEAS, TO
LIGHTER CHOICES, SUCH AS ROASTED AUBERGINES
STUFFED WITH FETA CHEESE AND FRESH CORIANDER
OR TOFU, ROASTED PEANUT AND PEPPER KEBABS,
THERE IS A DELICIOUS DISH FOR EVERYONE, WHETHER
VEGETARIAN OR NOT.

Vegetable Hot-pot ✳✳✳

Make this healthy one-dish meal in the summer, when the vegetables are in season, and serve with Italian bread, such as foccacia.

SERVES FOUR

1 Preheat the oven to 190°C/375°F/ Gas 5. Heat 45ml/3 tbsp of the oil in a heavy pan, and cook the onion until golden.

2 Add the aubergines, sauté for 3 minutes, then add the courgettes, peppers, peas, beans and potatoes, and stir in the spices and seasoning. Cook for 3 minutes, stirring constantly.

3 Cut the tomatoes in half and scoop out the seeds. Chop the tomatoes finely and place them in a bowl.

4 Stir in the canned tomatoes with the chopped fresh parsley, crushed garlic and the remaining olive oil.

5 Spoon the aubergine mixture into a shallow ovenproof dish and level the surface.

6 Pour the stock over the aubergine mixture and then spoon over the prepared tomato mixture.

7 Cover the dish with foil and bake for 30–45 minutes, until the vegetables are tender. Serve hot, garnished with black olives and parsley.

1 large onion, chopped

2 small or medium aubergines (eggplants), cut into small cubes

4 courgettes (zucchini), cut into small chunks

2 red, yellow or green (bell) peppers, seeded and chopped

115g/4oz/1 cup frozen peas

115g/4oz green beans

450g/1lb new or salad potatoes, peeled and cubed

4–5 tomatoes, peeled

30ml/2 tbsp chopped fresh parsley

3–4 garlic cloves, crushed

black olives and fresh parsley, to garnish

FROM THE STORECUPBOARD

60ml/4 tbsp extra virgin olive oil

200g/7oz can flageolet (small cannellini) beans, rinsed and drained

2.5ml/$\frac{1}{2}$ tsp ground cinnamon

2.5ml/$\frac{1}{2}$ tsp ground cumin

5ml/1 tsp paprika

400g/14oz can chopped tomatoes

350ml/12fl oz/1$\frac{1}{2}$ cups vegetable stock

salt and ground black pepper, to taste

Energy 386kcal/1618kJ; Protein 15.4g; Carbohydrate 51.7g, of which sugars 22.6g; Fat 14.5g, of which saturates 2.5g; Cholesterol 0mg; Calcium 142mg; Fibre 14.3g; Sodium 234mg

Hot and Spicy Parsnips and Chickpeas ✳✳

The sweet flavour of parsnips goes very well with the aromatic spices in this hearty and healthy Indian-style vegetable stew. Offer Indian breads such as naan to mop up the delicious sauce.

SERVES FOUR

7 garlic cloves, finely chopped

1 small onion, chopped

5cm/2in piece fresh root ginger, chopped

2 green chillies, seeded and finely chopped

450ml/³/₄ pint/scant 2 cups plus 75ml/5 tbsp water

50g/2oz cashew nuts, toasted and ground

250g/9oz tomatoes, peeled and chopped

900g/2lb parsnips, cut into chunks

juice of 1 lime, to taste

fresh coriander (cilantro) leaves, to garnish

cashew nuts, toasted, to garnish

FROM THE STORECUPBOARD

200g/7oz dried chickpeas, soaked overnight in cold water, then drained

60ml/4 tbsp vegetable oil

5ml/1 tsp cumin seeds

10ml/2 tsp ground coriander seeds

5ml/1 tsp ground turmeric

2.5–5ml/¹/₂–1 tsp chilli powder or mild paprika

5ml/1 tsp ground roasted cumin seeds

salt and ground black pepper, to taste

1 Put the soaked chickpeas in a pan, cover with cold water and bring to the boil. Boil vigorously for 10 minutes, then reduce the heat so that the water boils steadily, and cook for 1–1¹/₂ hours until the chickpeas are tender. Drain well.

2 Set 10ml/2 tsp of the garlic aside, then place the remainder in a food processor or blender with the onion, ginger and half the chillies. Add the 75ml/5 tbsp water and process to make a smooth paste.

3 Heat the oil in a large, deep, frying pan and cook the cumin seeds for 30 seconds. Stir in the coriander seeds, turmeric, chilli powder or paprika and the ground cashew nuts. Add the ginger and chilli paste and cook, stirring frequently, until the water begins to evaporate. Add the tomatoes and stir-fry until the mixture begins to turn red-brown in colour.

4 Mix in the chickpeas and parsnips with the rest of the water, the lime juice, 5ml/1 tsp salt and black pepper. Bring to the boil, stir, then simmer, uncovered, for 15–20 minutes, until the parsnips are completely tender.

5 Reduce the liquid until the sauce is thick. Add the ground roasted cumin. Stir in the reserved garlic and green chilli, and cook for a further 1–2 minutes. Sprinkle the coriander leaves and toasted cashew nuts over and serve immediately.

Energy 506kcal/2124kJ; Protein 18.4g; Carbohydrate 60.1g, of which sugars 18.2g; Fat 23.1g, of which saturates 3.4g; Cholesterol 0mg; Calcium 192mg; Fibre 17.1g; Sodium 86mg

Roasted Aubergines Stuffed with Feta Cheese and Fresh Coriander ✱✱✱

Aubergines take on a lovely smoky flavour when grilled on a barbecue. Choose a good-quality Greek feta cheese for the best flavour.

SERVES SIX

1 Prepare a barbecue. Cook the aubergines for 20 minutes on the barbecue, turning occasionally, until they are slightly charred and soft. Remove and cut in half lengthways.

2 Carefully scoop the aubergine flesh into a bowl, reserving the skins. Mash the flesh roughly with a fork.

3 Crumble the feta cheese, and then stir it into the mashed aubergine with the chopped coriander and olive oil. Season with salt and ground black pepper to taste.

4 Spoon the feta mixture back into the skins and return to the barbecue for 5 minutes to warm through.

5 Serve immediately with a fresh green salad coated with fruity extra virgin olive oil, garnished with sprigs of fresh coriander.

3 medium to large aubergines (eggplant)

400g/14oz feta cheese

a small bunch of fresh coriander (cilantro), roughly chopped, plus extra sprigs to garnish

FROM THE STORECUPBOARD

60ml/4 tbsp extra virgin olive oil

salt and ground black pepper

Energy 257Kcal/1,066kJ; Protein 12g; Carbohydrate 4.2g, of which sugars 3.9g; Fat 21.5g, of which saturates 10.3g; Cholesterol 47mg; Calcium 286mg; Fibre 3.3g; Sodium 968mg.

4 large onions

150g/5oz goat's cheese, crumbled or cubed

50g/2oz/1 cup fresh breadcrumbs

8 sun-dried tomatoes in oil, drained and chopped

1–2 garlic cloves, chopped

2.5ml/¹/₂ tsp chopped fresh thyme

30ml/2 tbsp chopped fresh parsley

1 small (US medium) egg, beaten

45ml/3 tbsp pine nuts, toasted

30ml/2 tbsp oil from the sun-dried tomatoes

FROM THE STORECUPBOARD

salt and ground black pepper, to taste

VARIATIONS

• *Use feta cheese in place of the goat's cheese and substitute mint, currants and pitted black olives for the other flavourings.*

• *Stuff the onions with wilted spinach and cooked long grain rice mixed with smoked mozzarella cheese and toasted flaked almonds.*

• *Substitute 175g/6oz Roquefort or Gorgonzola for the goat's cheese, omit the sun-dried tomatoes and pine nuts, and add 75g/3oz chopped walnuts and 115g/4oz chopped celery, cooked until soft with the chopped onion in 25ml/ 1¹/₂ tbsp olive oil.*

Onions Stuffed with Goat's Cheese and Sun-dried Tomatoes ✳✳

Roasted onions and tangy cheese are a winning combination. They make an excellent main course when served with rice.

SERVES FOUR

1 Bring a large pan of lightly salted water to the boil. Add the whole onions in their skins and boil for 10 minutes. Drain and cool, then cut each onion in half horizontally and peel.

2 Using a teaspoon, remove the centre of each onion, leaving a thick shell around the outside. Reserve the flesh and place the shells in an oiled ovenproof dish. Preheat the oven to 190°C/375°F/Gas 5.

3 Chop the scooped-out onion flesh and place in a bowl. Add the goat's cheese, breadcrumbs, sun-dried tomatoes, garlic, thyme, parsley and egg. Mix well, then season with salt and pepper and add the toasted pine nuts.

4 Divide the stuffing among the onions and cover with foil. Bake for about 25 minutes.

5 Uncover the onions, drizzle with the oil and cook for another 30–40 minutes, until bubbling and well cooked. Baste occasionally during cooking.

Energy 402kcal/1669kJ; Protein 14.8g; Carbohydrate 25.1g, of which sugars 11.7g; Fat 27.7g, of which saturates 8.8g; Cholesterol 82mg; Calcium 120mg; Fibre 3.2g; Sodium 346mg

Tofu and Green Bean Thai Red Curry ✳✳✳

This is one of those versatile recipes that should be in every cook's repertoire. This version uses green beans, but other types of vegetable work equally well, depending on what is available. The tofu takes on the flavour of the spice paste and also boosts the nutritional value.

SERVES FOUR

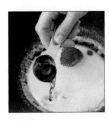

1 Pour about one-third of the coconut milk into a wok or large frying pan. Cook gently until it starts to separate and an oily sheen appears on the surface.

2 Add the red curry paste, fish sauce and sugar to the coconut milk. Mix thoroughly, then add the mushrooms. Stir and cook for 1 minute.

3 Stir in the remaining coconut milk. Bring back to the boil, then add the green beans and tofu cubes. Simmer gently for 4–5 minutes more.

4 Stir in the kaffir lime leaves and sliced red chillies. Spoon the curry into a serving dish, garnish with the coriander leaves and serve immediately.

600ml/1 pint/2¹/₂ cups canned coconut milk

15ml/1 tbsp Thai red curry paste

225g/8oz/3¹/₄ cups button (white) mushrooms

115g/4oz/scant 1 cup green beans, trimmed

175g/6oz firm tofu, rinsed, drained and cut in 2cm/³/₄in cubes

4 kaffir lime leaves, torn

2 fresh red chillies, seeded and sliced

fresh coriander (cilantro) leaves, to garnish

FROM THE STORECUPBOARD

45ml/3 tbsp Thai fish sauce

10ml/2 tsp light muscovado (brown) sugar

Energy 59kcal/250kJ; Protein 3.8g; Carbohydrate 7.5g, of which sugars 7.1g; Fat 1.8g, of which saturates 0.4g; Cholesterol 0mg; Calcium 188mg; Fibre 0.8g; Sodium 291mg

Tofu, Roasted Peanut and Pepper Kebabs ✳✳✳

A coating of ground, dry-roasted peanuts pressed on to cubed tofu provides plenty of flavour along with the peppers. Use metal or bamboo skewers for the kebabs – if you use bamboo, then soak them in cold water for 30 minutes before using, to prevent scorching.

SERVES FOUR

250g/9oz firm tofu, drained

50g/2oz/¹/₂ cup dry-roasted peanuts

2 red and 2 green (bell) peppers, halved and seeded

60ml/4 tbsp sweet chilli dipping sauce

1 Pat the tofu dry on kitchen paper, then cut it into small cubes. Finely grind the peanuts in a blender or food processor and transfer to a plate. Coat the tofu in the ground nuts.

2 Preheat the grill (broiler) to moderate. Cut the halved and seeded peppers into large chunks. Thread the chunks of pepper on to four large skewers with the tofu cubes and place on a foil-lined grill rack.

3 Grill (broil) the kebabs, turning them frequently, for 10–12 minutes, or until the peppers and peanuts are beginning to brown. Transfer the kebabs to plates and serve with the dipping sauce.

Energy 175kcal/730kJ; Protein 10g; Carbohydrate 12.9g, of which sugars 11.4g; Fat 9.6g, of which saturates 1.6g; Cholesterol 0mg; Calcium 339mg; Fibre 3.6g; Sodium 108mg

Salads and Side Dishes

WHETHER YOU WANT A LIGHT SALAD FOR A SUMMER LUNCH OR A TASTY ACCOMPANIMENT FOR A MAIN MEAL, THERE IS A DISH HERE TO SUIT YOU. CHOOSE FROM SUBSTANTIAL SALADS SUCH AS GRILLED AUBERGINE, MINT AND COUSCOUS SALAD OR GADO GADO SALAD, WHICH CAN BE SERVED ON THEIR OWN, OR WHY NOT MAKE A MEAL EXTRA SPECIAL WITH A DELECTABLE SIDE DISH, SUCH AS RADICCHIO AND CHICORY GRATIN OR BAKED WINTER SQUASH WITH TOMATOES?

Spiced Aubergine Salad with Yogurt and Parsley **

The delicate flavours of aubergine, tomatoes and cucumber are lightly spiced with cumin and coriander in this fresh-tasting salad. Make it in the summer, when the vegetables are at their best, and serve with bread.

SERVES FOUR

1 Preheat the grill (broiler). Lightly brush the aubergine slices with olive oil and cook them under a high heat, turning once, until they are golden and tender. Alternatively, cook them on a griddle pan.

2 When they are done, remove the aubergine slices to a chopping board and cut them into quarters.

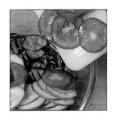

3 Mix together the remaining oil, the vinegar, garlic, lemon juice, cumin and coriander. Season with salt and pepper to taste and mix thoroughly.

4 Add the warm aubergines to the bowl, stir well and chill for at least 2 hours. Add the cucumber and tomatoes.

5 Transfer to a serving dish and spoon the yogurt on top. Sprinkle with parsley and serve with warm crusty bread.

2 small aubergines (eggplants), sliced

2 garlic cloves, crushed

15ml/1 tbsp lemon juice

$^1/_2$ cucumber, thinly sliced

2 well-flavoured tomatoes, thinly sliced

30ml/2 tbsp natural (plain) yogurt

chopped fresh flat leaf parsley, to garnish

FROM THE STORECUPBOARD

75ml/5 tbsp extra virgin olive oil

50ml/2fl oz/$^1/_4$ cup red wine vinegar

2.5ml/$^1/_2$ tsp ground cumin

2.5ml/$^1/_2$ tsp ground coriander

salt and ground black pepper, to taste

Energy 155Kcal/642kJ; Protein 1.9g; Carbohydrate 4.9g, of which sugars 4.7g; Fat 14.4g, of which saturates 2.2g; Cholesterol 0mg; Calcium 35mg; Fibre 2.7g; Sodium 14mg

Grilled Aubergine, Mint and Couscous Salad ✳✳

Packets of flavoured couscous are available in most supermarkets – you can use whichever you like, but garlic and coriander is particularly good for this recipe. Serve with a crisp green salad.

SERVES TWO

1 large aubergine (eggplant)

110g/4oz packet flavoured couscous

30ml/2 tbsp chopped fresh mint

FROM THE STORECUPBOARD

30ml/2 tbsp olive oil

salt and ground black pepper, to taste

1 Preheat the grill (broiler) to high. Cut the aubergine into large chunky pieces and toss them with the olive oil.

2 Season with salt and pepper to taste and spread the aubergine pieces on a non-stick baking sheet.

3 Grill the aubergine pieces for 5–6 minutes, turning occasionally, until they are golden brown.

4 Meanwhile, prepare the couscous according to the instructions on the packet.

5 Stir the grilled aubergine and chopped mint into the couscous, toss thoroughly and serve immediately with a crisp green salad.

Energy 251kcal/1044kJ; Protein 4.8g; Carbohydrate 32.5g, of which sugars 2g; Fat 12.1g, of which saturates 1.7g; Cholesterol 0mg; Calcium 53mg; Fibre 2g; Sodium 5mg

Warm Black-eyed Bean Salad ✳✳

This is an easy dish, as black-eyed beans do not need to be soaked overnight. By adding spring onions and dill, it is transformed into a refreshing and healthy meal. It can be served hot or cold.

SERVES FOUR

1 Thoroughly rinse the beans and drain them well. Tip into a pan and pour in cold water to just about cover them. Slowly bring to the boil over a low heat. As soon as the water is boiling, remove from the heat and drain the water off immediately.

2 Put the beans back in the pan with fresh cold water to cover and add a pinch of salt – this will make their skins harder and stop them from disintegrating when they are cooked.

3 Bring the beans to the boil over a medium heat, then lower the heat and cook them until they are soft but not mushy. They will take 20–30 minutes only, so keep an eye on them.

4 Drain the beans, reserving 75–90ml/5–6 tbsp of the cooking liquid. Tip the beans into a large salad bowl. Immediately add the remaining ingredients, including the reserved liquid, and mix well.

5 Serve immediately, piled on the lettuce leaves, or leave to cool slightly and serve later.

5 spring onions (scallions), sliced into rounds

a large handful of fresh rocket (arugula) leaves, chopped if large

45–60ml/3–4 tbsp chopped fresh dill

juice of 1 lemon, or to taste

10–12 black olives

small cos or romaine lettuce leaves, to serve

FROM THE STORECUPBOARD

275g/10oz/1¹/₂ cups black-eyed beans (peas)

150ml/¹/₄ pint/²/₃ cup extra virgin olive oil

salt and ground black pepper, to taste

Energy 434Kcal/1,811kJ; Protein 16.6g; Carbohydrate 31.4g, of which sugars 2.7g; Fat 27.8g, of which saturates 4g; Cholesterol 0mg; Calcium 149mg; Fibre 12.5g; Sodium 334mg.

225g/8oz new potatoes, scrubbed and halved

2 carrots, cut into sticks

115g/4oz green beans

¹/₂ small cauliflower, broken into florets

¹/₄ firm white cabbage, shredded

200g/7oz bean or lentil sprouts

4 eggs, hard-boiled and quartered

bunch of watercress (optional)

FOR THE SAUCE

90ml/6 tbsp crunchy peanut butter

300ml/¹/₂ pint/1¹/₄ cups cold water

1 garlic clove, crushed

15ml/1 tbsp dry sherry

15ml/1 tbsp fresh lemon juice

5ml/1 tsp anchovy essence (extract)

FROM THE STORECUPBOARD

30ml/2 tbsp dark soy sauce

10ml/2 tsp caster (superfine) sugar

COOK'S TIP

There is a range of nut butters available in health-food stores and supermarkets. Alternatively, make your own peanut butter by blending 225g/8oz/ 2 cups peanuts with 120ml/4fl oz/¹/₂ cup oil in a food processor.

Gado Gado Salad ✳✳

This Indonesian salad combines lightly steamed vegetables and hard-boiled eggs with a richly flavoured peanut and soy sauce dressing.

SERVES SIX

1 Place the halved potatoes in a metal colander or steamer and set over a pan of gently boiling water. Cover the pan or steamer with a lid and cook the potatoes for 10 minutes.

2 Add the rest of the vegetables to the steamer and steam for a further 10 minutes, until tender.

3 Cool and arrange on a platter with the egg quarters and the watercress, if using.

4 Beat together the peanut butter, water, garlic, sherry, lemon juice, anchovy essence, soy sauce and sugar in a large mixing bowl until smooth. Drizzle a little sauce over each portion then pour the rest into a small bowl and serve separately.

Energy 235kcal/979kJ; Protein 12.7g; Carbohydrate 18.3g, of which sugars 10.6g; Fat 12.5g, of which saturates 3.2g; Cholesterol 127mg; Calcium 91mg; Fibre 4.8g; Sodium 494mg

Radicchio and Chicory Gratin ✳✳

Baking seasonal salad vegetables in a creamy sauce creates a dish that is wholesome, warming and sustaining. It is delicious served with grilled meat or fish, or with a bean or lentil casserole.

SERVES FOUR

1 Preheat the oven to 180°C/350°F/Gas 4. Grease a 1.2 litre/ 2 pint/5 cup ovenproof dish and arrange the radicchio and chicory in it.

2 Sprinkle over the sun-dried tomatoes and brush the vegetables with oil from the jar.

3 Season to taste and cover with foil. Bake for 15 minutes, then uncover and bake for a further 10 minutes.

4 To make the sauce, place the butter in a small pan and melt over a medium heat. When it is foaming, add the flour and cook for 1 minute, stirring.

5 Remove from the heat and gradually add the milk, whisking all the time until smooth.

6 Return to the heat and bring to the boil, then simmer for 3 minutes to thicken. Season to taste and add the nutmeg.

7 Pour the sauce over the vegetables and sprinkle with the cheese. Bake for about 20 minutes. Serve immediately.

2 heads radicchio, quartered lengthways

2 heads chicory (Belgian endive), quartered lengthways

25g/1oz/¹/₂ cup drained sun-dried tomatoes in oil, coarsely chopped

25g/1oz/2 tbsp butter

250ml/8fl oz/1 cup milk

50g/2oz/¹/₂ cup grated Emmenthal cheese

FROM THE STORECUPBOARD

15g/¹/₂oz/2 tbsp plain (all-purpose) flour

pinch of freshly grated nutmeg

salt and ground black pepper, to taste

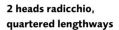

VARIATION *You could use fennel in place of the radicchio and chicory. Par-boil the fennel before putting it in the ovenproof dish, then continue as in the recipe.*

Energy 159kcal/662kJ; Protein 6.3g; Carbohydrate 8g, of which sugars 4.4g; Fat 11.6g, of which saturates 6.9g; Cholesterol 29mg; Calcium 196mg; Fibre 1g; Sodium 158mg

Baked Winter Squash with Tomatoes ✴

Acorn, butternut or Hubbard squash can all be used in this simple recipe. Serve the squash as a light main course, with warm crusty bread, or as a side dish for grilled meat or poultry.

SERVES SIX

1 Preheat the oven to 160°C/325°F/Gas 3. Heat the oil in a large frying pan and cook the pumpkin or squash slices, in batches, until they are golden brown. Remove them from the pan and set them aside as they are cooked.

2 Add the tomatoes to the pan and cook over a medium-high heat for 10 minutes, or until the mixture is of a thick sauce consistency. Stir in the rosemary and season to taste with salt and ground black pepper.

3 Layer the pumpkin slices and tomatoes in an ovenproof dish, ending with a layer of tomatoes.

4 Bake for 35 minutes, or until the top is lightly glazed and beginning to turn golden brown, and the pumpkin is tender. Serve immediately.

1kg/2¼lb pumpkin or orange winter squash, peeled and sliced

2–3 fresh rosemary sprigs, stems removed and leaves chopped

FROM THE STORECUPBOARD

45ml/3 tbsp garlic-flavoured olive oil

2 x 400g/14oz cans chopped tomatoes

salt and ground black pepper, to taste

Energy 94kcal/392kJ; Protein 2.1g; Carbohydrate 7.8g, of which sugars 7g; Fat 6.2g, of which saturates 1.1g; Cholesterol 0mg; Calcium 58mg; Fibre 3g; Sodium 12mg

Potatoes and Parsnips Baked with Garlic and Cream ✳

This creamy, flavoursome baked dish is the ideal accompaniment to any number of main course dishes and is particularly good during the winter months. As the potatoes and parsnips cook, they gradually absorb the garlic-flavoured cream, while the cheese browns to a crispy finish.

3 large potatoes, total weight about 675g/1¹/₂lb

350g/12oz small–medium parsnips

200ml/7fl oz/scant 1 cup single (light) cream

105ml/7 tbsp milk

2 garlic cloves, crushed

butter or olive oil, for greasing

75g/3oz/³/₄ cup coarsely grated Cheddar cheese

FROM THE STORECUPBOARD

about 5ml/1 tsp freshly grated nutmeg

salt and ground black pepper, to taste

COOK'S TIPS

• If you have one, use a mandolin or a food processor fitted with a slicing blade to slice the potatoes and parsnips thinly and evenly.

• At the end of the cooking time, to test if the vegetables are tender, insert a sharp knife through the middle of the potatoes and parsnips. The knife should slide in easily, and the vegetables should feel soft. If not, give them a few more minutes.

1 Peel the potatoes and parsnips and cut them into thin slices using a sharp knife. Place them in a steamer and cook for 5 minutes. Leave to cool slightly.

2 Meanwhile, pour the cream and milk into a heavy pan, add the crushed garlic and bring to the boil over a medium heat.

3 Remove the pan from the heat and leave to stand at room temperature for about 10 minutes to allow the flavour of the garlic to infuse into the cream and milk mixture.

4 Lightly grease a 25cm/10in long, shallow rectangular earthenware baking dish with butter or oil. Preheat the oven to 180 °C/350°F/Gas 4.

5 Arrange the thinly sliced potatoes and parsnips in layers in the greased earthenware dish, sprinkling each layer of vegetables with a little freshly grated nutmeg, a little salt and plenty of ground black pepper.

6 Pour the cream and milk mixture into the dish and then press the sliced potatoes and parsnips down into the liquid. The liquid should come to just underneath the top layer of vegetables.

7 Cover the dish with a piece of lightly buttered foil or baking parchment and bake for 45 minutes.

8 Remove the dish from the oven and remove the foil or paper from the dish. Sprinkle the grated Cheddar cheese over the vegetables in an even layer.

9 Return the dish to the oven and bake uncovered for a further 20–30 minutes, or until the potatoes and parsnips are tender and the topping is golden brown.

VARIATION

You can use orange-fleshed sweet potatoes in place of some or all of the ordinary potatoes for a delicious and sustaining alternative. Other root vegetables such as Jerusalem artichokes, carrots, swede (rutabaga) or turnips would also work well in combination with the potato.

Energy 1443kcal/6055kJ; Protein 47g; Carbohydrate 161.8g, of which sugars 38.1g; Fat 70.4g, of which saturates 43.1g; Cholesterol 189mg; Calcium 1042mg; Fibre 22.8g; Sodium 755mg

Delectable Desserts

HOME-MADE DESSERTS ARE THE PERFECT WAY TO
FINISH ANY MEAL AND ARE SURE TO BE POPULAR WITH
EVERYONE. THIS CHAPTER CONTAINS A SELECTION OF
THE VERY BEST, RANGING FROM COMFORTING WINTER
WARMERS SUCH AS HOT CHOCOLATE PUDDING WITH
RUM CUSTARD OR BREAD AND BUTTER PUDDING
WITH WHISKEY SAUCE, TO LIGHTER ONES THAT
MAKE GOOD USE OF SEASONAL FRUITS, SUCH AS
MERINGUE LAYER CAKE WITH RASPBERRIES OR
FRESH FIG COMPOTE.

Hot Chocolate Pudding with Rum Custard ✳

These delicious chocolate puddings are sure to be a hit. The rum custard turns them into a more adult pudding; for a family dessert, flavour the custard with vanilla or orange rind instead, if you like.

SERVES SIX

1 Lightly grease a 1.2 litre/2 pint/5 cup heatproof bowl or six individual dariole moulds. Cream the butter and sugar until pale and creamy. Gently blend in the eggs and the vanilla extract.

2 Sift together the cocoa powder and flour, and fold gently into the egg mixture with the chopped chocolate and sufficient milk to give a soft dropping consistency.

3 Spoon the mixture into the basin or moulds, cover with buttered greaseproof paper and tie down. Fill a pan with 2.5–5cm/1–2in water, place the puddings in the pan, cover with a lid and bring to the boil. Steam the large pudding for 1^1/$_2$–2 hours and the individual puddings for 45–50 minutes, topping up the pan with water if necessary. When firm, turn out on to warm plates.

4 To make the rum custard, bring the milk and sugar to the boil. Whisk together the egg yolks and cornflour, then pour on the hot milk, whisking constantly. Return the mixture to the pan and stir continuously while it slowly comes back to the boil. Allow the sauce to simmer gently as it thickens, stirring all the time. Remove from the heat and stir in the rum.

115g/4oz/^{1}/$_2$ cup butter, plus extra for greasing

2 eggs, beaten

drops of vanilla extract

45ml/3 tbsp unsweetened cocoa powder, sifted

75g/3oz bitter (semisweet) chocolate, chopped

a little milk, warmed

FOR THE RUM CUSTARD

250ml/8fl oz/1 cup milk

2 egg yolks

30–45ml/2–3 tbsp rum

FROM THE STORECUPBOARD

115g/4oz/^{1}/$_2$ cup soft light brown sugar

115g/4oz/1 cup self-raising (self-rising) flour

15ml/1 tbsp caster (superfine) sugar

10ml/2 tsp cornflour (cornstarch)

Energy 458Kcal/1915kJ; Protein 8.3g; Carbohydrate 49g, of which sugars 31.5g; Fat 25.6g, of which saturates 14.5g; Cholesterol 186mg; Calcium 145mg; Fibre 1.8g; Sodium 302mg

Bread and Butter Pudding with Whiskey Sauce ✳

This traditional dessert is a great way of using up stale white bread. The whiskey sauce is heavenly, but the pudding can also be served with chilled cream or vanilla ice cream, if you prefer.

SERVES SIX

8 slices of white bread, buttered

115–150g/4–5oz/ ²/₃–³/₄ cup sultanas (golden raisins), or mixed dried fruit

2 large (US extra large) eggs

300ml/¹/₂ pint/1¹/₄ cups single (light) cream

450ml/³/₄ pint/ scant 2 cups milk

5ml/1 tsp of vanilla essence (extract)

FOR THE WHISKEY SAUCE

150g/5oz/10 tbsp butter

1 egg

45ml/3 tbsp Irish whiskey

FROM THE STORECUPBOARD

2.5ml/¹/₂ tsp grated nutmeg

260g/9¹/₂oz/1¹/₄ cups caster (superfine) sugar

light muscovado (brown) sugar, for sprinkling (optional)

1 Preheat the oven to 180°C/350°F/Gas 4. Remove the crusts from the bread and put four slices, buttered side down, in the base of an ovenproof dish. Sprinkle with the sultanas or mixed dried fruit, some of the nutmeg and 15ml/1 tbsp sugar.

2 Place the remaining four slices of bread on top, buttered side down, and sprinkle again with nutmeg and 15ml/1 tbsp sugar.

3 Beat the eggs, add the cream, milk, vanilla essence and 115g/4oz/generous ¹/₂ cup caster sugar, and mix well to make a custard. Pour over the bread, and sprinkle light muscovado sugar over the top, if you like to have a crispy crust. Bake for 1 hour, or until the pudding has risen and is brown.

4 Meanwhile, make the whiskey sauce: melt the butter in a heavy pan, add the remaining caster sugar and dissolve over a gentle heat. Remove from the heat and add the egg, whisking vigorously, and then add the whiskey. Serve the pudding on hot serving plates, with the whiskey sauce poured over the top.

Energy 757Kcal/3168kJ; Protein 11.7g; Carbohydrate 82g, of which sugars 65.2g; Fat 40.8g, of which saturates 24.3g; Cholesterol 207mg; Calcium 232mg; Fibre 0.9g; Sodium 472mg

Meringue Layer Cake with Raspberries ✳

This delicious dessert is made with a basic meringue mixture, and is the perfect way to enjoy raspberries, or any other soft fruit, depending on availability and personal preference. Making meringues is a great way of using up eggs that are not absolutely fresh or any egg whites left over from another recipe.

SERVES TEN

1 Preheat the oven to 150°C/300°F/Gas 2. Line two baking sheets with non-stick baking parchment and draw two circles: one 23cm/9in in diameter and the other 20cm/8in. Fit a piping (icing) bag with a 1cm/^{1}/$_2$in star nozzle.

2 Whisk the egg whites until stiff peaks form, using an electric mixer. Keeping the machine running, add half of the sugar, 15ml/1 tbsp at a time. Carefully fold in the remaining sugar. Use most of the mixture to pipe inside the circles, then use the remainder to pipe nine miniature meringues.

3 Cook for 50–60 minutes, until lightly coloured and dry (the small ones will take less time). Peel off the parchment, cool on wire racks and, when cold, store in airtight containers.

4 Whip the cream until soft peaks form, sweeten with sugar and flavour with a few drops of vanilla extract or liqueur.

5 Lay the larger meringue on a serving dish. Spread with most of the cream and raspberries. Add the smaller meringue, spread with the remaining cream, and arrange the small meringues around the edge. Decorate the top with the remaining fruit and dust lightly with icing sugar.

4 egg whites

FOR THE FILLING

300ml/^{1}/$_2$ pint/1^1/$_4$ cups whipping cream

3–4 drops of vanilla extract or 2.5ml/^{1}/$_2$ tsp liqueur, such as Kirsch or Crème de Framboise

about 450g/1lb/2^3/$_4$ cups raspberries

FROM THE STORECUPBOARD

225g/8oz/generous 1 cup caster (superfine) sugar, plus extra, to taste

icing (confectioners') sugar, for dusting

Energy 298Kcal/1252kJ; Protein 3.2g; Carbohydrate 39.5g, of which sugars 39.5g; Fat 15.3g, of which saturates 9.5g; Cholesterol 39mg; Calcium 55mg; Fibre 1.4g; Sodium 44mg

Autumn Pudding ✳

Although summer pudding is made more often, this pudding is equally easy to make, using autumnal fruit instead of the soft fruits of summer. This juicy dessert is very simple to make, but it looks superb. Serve with lightly whipped chilled cream, or crème fraîche.

SERVES EIGHT

1 loaf white bread, 2 or 3 days old

675g/1¹/₂lb/6 cups mixed soft fruit, such as blackberries and peeled, chopped eating apples

FROM THE STORECUPBOARD

115g/4oz/generous ¹/₂ cup caster (superfine) sugar

1 Remove the crusts from the loaf and slice the bread thinly. Use several slices to line the base and sides of a 900ml–1.2 litre/1¹/₂–2 pint/3³/₄–5 cup pudding bowl or soufflé dish, cutting them so that the pieces fit closely together.

2 Put all the fruit into a wide, heavy pan, sprinkle the sugar over and bring very gently to the boil. Cook for 2–3 minutes, or until the sugar has dissolved and the juices run.

3 Remove the pan from the heat and set aside 30–45ml/2–3 tbsp of the juices. Spoon the fruit and the remaining juices into the prepared bread-lined dish and cover the top closely with the remaining slices of bread. Put a plate that fits neatly inside the top of the dish on top of the pudding and weigh it down with a heavy can or jar. Leave in the refrigerator for at least 8 hours, or overnight.

4 Before serving the dish, remove the weight and plate, cover the bowl with a serving plate and turn upside down to unmould the pudding.

5 Use the reserved fruit juice to pour over any patches of the bread that have not been completely soaked and coloured by the fruit juices. Serve cold, cut into wedges with lightly whipped chilled cream or crème fraîche.

Energy 261Kcal/1112kJ; Protein 7.7g; Carbohydrate 57.5g, of which sugars 27.1g; Fat 1.7g, of which saturates 0.4g; Cholesterol 0mg; Calcium 153mg; Fibre 4.2g; Sodium 398mg

Oranges in Syrup ✳

This recipe works well with most citrus fruits – for example, try pink grapefruit or sweet, perfumed clementines, which have been peeled but left whole. Serve the oranges with 300ml/½ pint/1¼ cups whipped cream flavoured with 5ml/1 tsp ground cinnamon, or 5ml/1 tsp ground nutmeg or with Greek (US strained plain) yogurt for an elegant summer dessert.

SERVES SIX

6 medium oranges

100ml/3½fl oz/ scant ½ cup fresh strong brewed coffee

50g/2oz/½ cup pistachio nuts, chopped (optional)

FROM THE STORECUPBOARD

200g/7oz/1 cup sugar

1 Finely pare, shred and reserve the rind from one orange. Peel the remaining oranges. Cut each crossways into slices, then re-form them, with a cocktail stick (toothpick) through the centre.

2 Put the sugar in a heavy pan and add 50ml/2fl oz/¼ cup water. Heat gently until the sugar dissolves, then bring to the boil and cook until the syrup turns pale gold.

3 Remove from the heat and carefully pour 100ml/3½fl oz/ scant ½ cup freshly boiling water into the pan. Return to the heat until the syrup has dissolved in the water. Stir in the coffee.

4 Add the oranges and the rind to the coffee syrup. Simmer for 15–20 minutes, turning the oranges once during cooking. Leave to cool, then chill. Serve sprinkled with pistachio nuts, if using.

Fresh Fig Compote ✳✳✳

A vanilla and coffee syrup brings out the wonderful flavour of figs. Serve Greek (US strained plain) yogurt or vanilla ice cream with the poached fruit. A good selection of different honeys is available – the aroma and flavour will be subtly scented by the plants surrounding the hives. Orange blossom honey works particularly well in this recipe, although any clear variety is suitable.

SERVES SIX

400ml/14fl oz/ 1⅔ cups fresh brewed coffee

115g/4oz/½ cup clear honey

1 vanilla pod (bean)

12 slightly under-ripe fresh figs

1 Choose a frying pan with a lid, large enough to hold the figs in a single layer. Pour in the coffee and add the honey.

2 Split the vanilla pod lengthways and scrape the seeds into the pan. Add the vanilla pod, then bring to a rapid boil and cook until reduced to about 175ml/6fl oz/¾ cup.

3 Wash the figs and pierce the skins several times with a sharp skewer. Cut in half and add to the syrup. Reduce the heat, cover and simmer for 5 minutes. Remove the figs from the syrup with a slotted spoon and set aside to cool.

4 Strain the syrup over the figs. Allow to stand at room temperature for 1 hour before serving.

COOK'S TIP *Figs come in three main varieties – red, white and black – and all three are suitable for cooking. They are sweet and succulent, and complement the stronger, more pervasive flavours of coffee and vanilla very well.*

Top: Energy 191kcal/815kJ; Protein 2g; Carbohydrate 48.5g, of which sugars 48.5g; Fat 0.2g, of which saturates 0g; Cholesterol 0mg; Calcium 93mg; Fibre 2.7g; Sodium 10mg

Above: Energy 147kcal/628kJ; Protein 1.7g; Carbohydrate 36g, of which sugars 35.8g; Fat 0.6g, of which saturates 0g; Cholesterol 0mg; Calcium 103mg; Fibre 3g; Sodium 27mg

Index